Walk With God Today

Christian Devotional

◆

By Coach Brian Williams

INSPIRED LIFE PUBLISHING

CALIFORNIA

Walk With God Today
Christian Daily Devotional

Copyright © Brian Williams 2012 All rights reserved. No part of this book may be reproduced, stored in a retrieval system, or transmitted in any form, without the written permission of Brian Williams

Published by:

ISBN 978-0-9856953-0-9

All scripture quotations, unless otherwise indicated, are taken from the Holy Bible, New International Version®, NIV®. Copyright ©1973, 1978, 1984, 2011 by Biblica, Inc.TM Used by permission of Zondervan. All rights reserved worldwide. www.zondervan.com The "NIV" and "New International Version" are trademarks registered in the United States Patent and Trademark Office by Biblica, Inc.TM

Proofread by Dale Williams
Final manuscript review by Erik Landvik
Design by Phil Moffitt
Cover photo by Claudia Williams

Printed and bound in the United States of America

Table of Contents

About The Author 5

Preface (Important) 6

How To Use This Book 7

Do You Know Jesus? 8

Aknowledgements 11

Testimonials 12

In Loving Memory 13

Foreword 14

Chapters:

  1 Exceptional *(2 Peter 1)* 15

  2 Fear Not *(Mark 4:40)* 17

  3 Use Your GPS *(Jeremiah 29:11-13)* 19

  4 What's The Good Word? *(Hebrews 4:12)* 21

  5 Living The Life *(Revelation 21:7-8)* 23

  6 Being A Man *(1 Timothy 1)* 25

  7 Beautiful *(Proverbs 31:29)* 27

  8 The Closing Ceremony *(Revelation 21:4-7)* 29

  9 What Are You Doing Today? *(Romans 14:23)* 31

 10 Take Inventory *(Colossians 3:23)* 33

 11 Your Life Adventure *(Hebrews 11:1)* 35

 12 Life's Hurricanes *(Matthew 7:25)* 37

 13 Your Personal Economy *(Proverbs 22:7)* 39

 14 Get Out Of Your Boat *(Matthew 14:22-25)* 41

 15 Fear Not! *(Isaiah 41:13)* 43

 16 Staying Young *(Luke 18:16-17)* 45

 17 Personal Development *(Proverbs 14:12)* 47

 18 Do The Last Thing God Showed You! *(Exodus 14:12)* 49

19	Trusting Jesus *(Romans 8:28–30)*	51
20	Real Christianity *(Acts 11:26)*	53
21	Crash! *(Romans 8:39)*	55
22	How True It Is *(Joshua 1:8)*	57
23	How To Really Communicate *(Matthew 6:9–13)*	59
24	Through Christ *(Philippians 4:13)*	61
25	Perfect Storms *(Matthew 11:28–30)*	63
26	What Are You Waiting For? *(Romans 14:23)*	65
27	Joyful Trials *(James 1:2–4)*	67
28	Never Give Up! *(Revelation 21:7)*	69
29	Why Me Lord? *(Philippians 2:5)*	71
30	Special Guest *(1 Corinthians 3:16–17)*	73
31	Listen *(Psalm 65:2–4)*	75
32	I Love You! *(Matthew 22:36–40)*	77
33	Growing Up *(1 Peter 1:5–11)*	79
34	How To Fix A Country! *(2 Chronicles 7:13–15)*	81
35	Love Who? *(Luke 6:35)*	83
36	Most Important *(1 John 2:17)*	85
37	You're Asking For It *(James 5:16)*	87
38	On Guard! *(1 Peter 5:8)*	89
39	How Hard Could It Really Be? *(2 Corinthians 10:5)*	91
40	Your Greatest Fan *(Ecclesiastes 3:1)*	93
41	How To Grow Up – Spiritually! *(Hebrews 5:12–14)*	95
42	Not So Beautiful *(1 John 5:14)*	97
43	Then What? *(Matthew 6:19–20)*	99
44	Unity *(Colossians 3:1–4)*	101
45	Top Priority *(Matthew 28:18–20)*	103
46	Wake Up *(2 Corinthians 4:16–18)*	105
47	Significant *(Ephesians 2:10)*	107
48	Guess Whats Blocking Your View? *(Hebrews 4:13)*	109
49	Making Tough Decisions *(Hebrews 11:6)*	111
50	The "Why's" & "How's" Of Being A Christian *(Proverbs 29:18)*	113
51	Fight Versus Flight *(Ephesians 6:12)*	115
52	Know That You Know *(Matthew 25:21)*	117

About the Author

Brian Williams is a Board Certified Coach and has extensive experience in helping many improve key areas of their lives including wellness, career, business, relationships, and most importantly, walking with Jesus. He has assisted more than 1,000 people in these different areas and has helped many of them fulfill their God ordained purpose through the direction of Jesus Christ. He partners with each person to help him (or her) clearly move forward by taking the right steps, and, through accountability and encouragement, to achieve those goals.

Brian also is an ordained pastor through the Anchor Bay Evangelistic Association. He uses his spiritual background and training not only to help others grow through coaching but also to help lead the Prayer Ministry at his church, facilitate small groups and organize various spiritual campaigns and church projects. Brian and his wife Claudia attend and serve at Saddleback Community Church in Southern California.

Preface | IMPORTANT!

Just like any instructional or devotional book, this one can be just informational or literally transformational! It is really up to you based on how you want to use it. At a minimum this book will get you thinking about the importance of your life, your walk with God and how you live today in light of eternity. It will cause you to think about how you are living and thinking, and whether or not you are having the greatest adventure and fulfilled life Jesus Christ has planned for you.

At its most effective level, this book will cause you to look deep into the core of who you are and who God is, and it will change and transform your thinking and your life as you walk day by day, step by step and moment by moment. This will lead you to the greatest adventure of your life and also an eternity with many others whom you have impacted and touched along the way for the sake of Jesus Christ.

My background (of helping well over a thousand people through hands-on coaching, mentoring and teaching) has prepared me for the writing of this book. I personally have made big shifts and changes in my life and thinking as I have been led by God, and because of this, have the opportunity to help a great number of others change their lives as well. Through all this I realized we are all exactly the same – at the core of each of us it the desire to be loved, to know God and to fulfill his purpose. Unfortunately, many people, including Christians don't live or experience these things fully in their own lives. I am here to say that you can and you will if you are steadfast in your pursuit of God and His purpose for your life. I have provided some help and support through this book to lead you to achieve just that.

It is important to understand that living fully for Christ does not mean your life will every day be free of challenges, obstacles or even very difficult situations. It does mean that you will have success (the way God defines it), complete fulfillment, incredible adventure, and the greatest news of all, the opportunity at the end of your life to hear your Lord and Father, the creator of you and all the universe say, "Well done good and faithful servant!"

How To Use This Book

The reason I have written this book is because Jesus Christ has transformed me and given me hope in place of my hopelessness. Now I am compelled and called by Him to give back to others as He and so many others have given to me.

I have realized through the process of my life changes, and in helping other people with theirs that we all learn and grow differently! However, deep down we all want to walk with God and fulfill His calling and purpose. I have found that in helping a large number of people make life style changes that change starts with awareness and as that awareness becomes stronger it turns into desire which then leads to action. This all happens in our lives at different times and rates of speed, but the most effective way to get started is by following simple, easy to understand concepts and examples.

This book is designed and recommended to be used as a one year devotional which can have a powerful impact on your spiritual life. Described below is how to read, absorb and put into practice what you read over a year's time. You may want to read a full chapter a day (spending whatever time you desire on the questions and action steps) or you may want to take two or three days per chapter (dividing the sections up as you wish). The best question for you to ask yourself in deciding how to use this book is the following: Does the plan I am choosing improve my walk with Jesus to the extent that I will be able to hear Him say at the end of each day "Well done good and faithful servant"?

The 52 "chapters" in this book are meditations using stories, illustrations and key biblical principles. They are designed to make you not only think, but also to consider how each one applies to you and what you can (or will) adjust in your life to walk closer with Christ. There is also a prayer for each chapter that goes directly with the meditation to help you connect with God in this specific area of your life.

You will find the two following sections ("Coaching Questions" and "Action Plan") are specifically designed to help you take your life and spiritual walk to the next level. The Questions are designed to get you to think deeply about these areas of your life. The best way to use this section is to take time and answer them, ideally one per day, which is why there are 7 questions per chapter. Think through these questions and write your answers down. Don't allow yourself to give one word or superficial answers. If you will be truthful with yourself and your Lord, you will find these questions and answers not only to be full of impact, but over time, life changing.

Finally the "Action Plan" section is not only an accountability area to help you grow, but also an action step that you can make as simple or as challenging as you feel God is leading you to take. By actually committing to a change, then taking steps to make that change you will find you will grow and become more Christ like day by day. I guarantee if you interact continually by not only reading and praying through the material, but also by truthfully asking the questions and taking the coaching tip challenges, you will grow in your spiritual walk with Christ!

It is also very important to note that this book is not designed to teach you to fly solo in life. It is designed to help you grow in your relationships with others, and to encourage you to ask another person to walk with you through these changes. As the Bible says, "man sharpens man like iron sharpens iron", which applies equally to men and women. A word of caution here, it is highly recommended that you have a same-sex accountability partner unless, of course, that person is your spouse or another family member.

Do You Know Jesus?

This book will be a great help for your walk with Jesus. However, I realize some of you reading this may not know what it means to be a Christian or even if you are one. This section is for you and will help you not only understand what being a Christian means but also help you make the most important decision in your life if you are ready.

I will start with my background and how I became a Christian. In my early 20's I graduated from college and moved to Florida. Even though I was already becoming successful at a young age, I found myself on Clearwater Beach one Saturday in a miserable state of mind. Even though I had grown up going to church I ended up hopeless and all the accomplishments, friends, church sermons and other things I had in life did not bring fulfillment. I asked myself what the purpose was in continuing to move forward in life.

When I got to my lowest low and sat on the beach that day, I looked around at the sky, the ocean and the birds flying, and realized that no man made what I saw and no man controls it. I knew I couldn't make it on my own and needed a bigger purpose and reason for life. I also knew what it meant to turn my life over to God, so I prayed to Jesus and surrendered my life to Him. I knew that I had sinned (missed the mark) many times in my life and asked Jesus to forgive me. I asked Jesus to give me His purpose and direction. I committed to pray and read the Bible every day and promised God that if He would help me out of my miserable mess, I would tell everyone I could about His love and forgiveness and about the transformation in my life. So here I am writing this to you because of this complete transformation of my life.

I have kept that commitment to spend daily time with Him each morning over the past 20 years. I can probably count on one hand the number of times I have missed praying and Bible reading. There were some big changes God walked me through over the months and years that followed my day at the beach including putting away my selfish desires, changing my focus, and my thinking in order to believe what is true based on what He says in the Bible. He empowers me to pursue a much bigger and more important purpose for my life here on earth and for eternity.

I have talked with many people and it is easy to see that what the Bible says is true – we all are in the same boat of having sinned in our lives. Sin is the opposite of God's will and is mainly formed from our selfish desires and attitudes. Sin includes things like anger, jealousy, bitterness, fear, unbelieving, immoral thoughts, sexuality outside of marriage, lying, wanting someone else's property and lust, just to name a few. It is putting yourself and "things" in life as the most important in the place of God. Sin is disobedience to God and the way he wants us to live and work together here on this earth through His love.

God not only has a plan for you here on earth, but also for eternity. The problem is sin separates us from God and causes a chasm between us. This is a chasm we cannot cross on our own because we are the ones that caused it. You may know that in the Old Testament of the Bible God required people to sacrifice animals to redeem their sins and bridge that chasm. That may sound harsh, but sin is so serious to God that its penalty is death. The payment for sin requires either our own personal death or the death of a substitute (in this case an animal).

The great news is that a couple thousand years ago God made a cataclysmic change by redeeming our sins and removing the separation from Him. He Himself, in the form of His son, Jesus, came to earth as a baby through a virgin named Mary. This is the real reason we celebrate Christmas. The story doesn't end there however.

After Jesus was born He walked the earth and was the only person to live a sinless life and follow God's purpose in every way. At 33 years old, Jesus was put to death by people alive in that day. For more details of the amazing life and events of Jesus' life, you can read the books of Matthew, Mark, Luke and John in the Bible.

Because of Jesus' life and death on the cross, He became the ultimate sacrifice and redemption for your sin. The most exciting part is three days later Jesus rose from the dead and was seen by hundreds of witnesses who not only saw Him, but also talked with Him and even touched his wounds. Jesus did not just die like a lot of other religious leaders who are still dead. He rose again and is alive today calling you to Him.

Jesus gave us a way to be forgiven through His sinless blood shed on a cross: He died in our place. You may be familiar with John 3:16, which says "For God so loved the world that He gave His only son so that whoever believes in Him will not perish but will have eternal life." Another verse in Romans 10 says "If you declare with your mouth, 'Jesus is Lord', and believe in your heart that God raised him from the dead, you will be saved. For it is with your heart that you believe and are justified, and it is with your mouth that you profess your faith and are saved."

This means that the most incredible thing God could ever do for you, he already did. This means that you don't have to try to face life on your own anymore but that you will be given a purpose and peace that you can never get anywhere else. It means that you want Him to lead and guide your life. It also means you want to be (and will be) with Him for eternity once you leave this earth. In order to bridge that chasm and have a relationship with your heavenly Father, all you have to do is believe. Believe that He died on the cross for you and ask Him to forgive your sins, which again are all the past things you have done wrong in your life. When you ask Him to come into your heart, He will, and He will change your life forever.

If you are ready to turn things over to God and live a full and adventurous life filled with peace and tremendous purpose for now and eternity, here is a prayer for you to pray out loud or in your heart.

"Jesus, I believe you are the son of God and that you died for my sins, then rose again. Thank you for loving me so much that you sacrificed your very life. I know that I have done things in my life that were against your will and purpose. Please forgive me. I want to start new with you! I ask you to come into my life and lead me. I want you to show me your way and the true purpose that you put me on this earth. Thank you Lord Jesus, I dedicate my life to you. Amen."

Congratulations!

You probably didn't have fireworks go off or hear a voice come down from heaven. You may not have felt anything inside either, but rest assured, God heard you and He is faithful. What you will probably notice right away, but certainly over time, is a peace inside your heart. You are now part of the family of God, which is a huge family of other believers you will be with for eternity.

It is important to share with someone the decision you made today. You can share it with family or friends. If you have another Christian in your life, I'm sure he or she would love to hear about your decision and so would I. Please e-mail me at coachbrianwilliams@gmail.com and let me know about your exciting decision. I can send you some additional resources to help you with your new life of following Jesus.

A next great step for you would be to attend a local church and/or Bible study group. Make sure the place you attend is using only the Holy Bible as their source of truth and training. Another great book you may want to pick up to help know more about what is next is called *The Purpose Driven Life* by Rick Warren.

Now you may have read all of this and not felt ready to make this change or commitment. I want you to know that God loves you more than you can comprehend! He is faithful and will keep tugging at your heart! If you have questions or need help sorting this out, please e-mail me at coachbrianwilliams@gmail.com. You may also find great answers and insight by reading the book listed above or *The Case for Christ* by Lee Strobel.

God bless you and remember that Jesus loves you so much that He died for you.

Acknowledgements

If you have read any of my testimonial above, you will quickly see I would not even be alive today if Jesus Christ hadn't saved and changed me. Without Christ's perfect will and plan I would not be here to write a book about how He has impacted my life. Thank you, Lord, for saving me through your mercy and grace on the beach that day and for daily leading me along your path through your Holy Spirit.

I would also be completely amiss if I did not thank my lovely wife Claudia. She is the one who has been with me through many of these stories in the devotionals you will read below. She has sacrificed along with me for this book as I got up many days early in the morning to write. She is my chief reader, critic and editor. Even more important is that she prays for me in my pursuit of God's call. Thank you Claudia: my other half. I love you!

There are so many others I would like to thank and acknowledge by name but that would turn this into an encyclopedia instead of one book. So I say from the bottom of my heart to my family and many friends who have supported me, encouraged me, and given me feedback over the years for my weekly message – Thank You! I cannot tell you how much your lives and encouragement mean to me.

Testimonials

Hey Brian, Great word!!! I am sure that it spoke loudly to many. Thanks for the blessing, *Bob*

Thank you from every part of my heart Brian! Love you both. *Andrea*

Thanks, brother Brian…Your encouraging devotions are helping a lot of people. *Linn*

Thank you for the encouraging words. … Ouch. It hit me, but it was a good hit. Keep up the good work. We all need life coaches to keep us fit for kingdom work. Your other posting was an answer to a prayer I have been asking. Thank you again for being obedient to what God is giving you to share with the body. *LARRY*

God is using you in more ways than you know. Thanks, *Jon*

This is so good, Brian! Thanks! *Jonathan*

While I sit here crying at my computer knowing full well God had me read this tonight. Thanks for God's timing and letting him use you. – *Andi*

You cannot even imagine the timing of this email (with a portion of the book). Thank you so much for following God's calling and sending these emails out because they truly help those who are really struggling sometimes with life. We were in the state of shock today and sad then I received this email from you….an answer from God that helped us both. He is so good. Again, please keep coming with these emails as you will never know who you will bless next! God is speaking through you! *Bev*

Thank you so much for those words of wisdom! They really help and I will use them continually as I pray. – *Scott*

The Holy Spirit seems to always allow you to share words of encouragement at the right time. I truly appreciate your passion for Christ and for taking time to spread the Gospel of Jesus, may God richest Blessings be upon you and your family. *Mona.*

I just want to thank you for your continuing to send your … thoughts. We always look forward to reading them. *Al & Cindy*

Thank you so much for all these inspiring words that you give to us all the time, you will never know how much of a blessing you are to the body of Christ around the globe. *Daniel*

Thanks Brian! The Holy Spirit knows what to say, when to say it, and who needs to hear it.
Your message is spot on! *Stuart*

Great story…! It really spoke to me and showed me something that I have been praying about for some time now. God is protecting me. *Cathy*

I started doing your devotional with my kids. It is going well. The action plans have been a perfect way for them to identify some areas in their lives that they need to address and pray about. It has spurred good conversation and has made them more self aware. Thought you might be interested to know.
Blessings, *Kaylene, John 10:10*

Foreword

In Jeremiah 29:11 we read, "For I know the plans I have for you," declares the Lord, "plans to prosper you and not harm you, plans to give you hope and a future." NIV

What great news for all of us. All we have to do is be open to the leading of the Holy Spirit and be obedient to his direction. Often that leading involves letting him speak to us through other people. I believe very strongly that one of those people, if you're reading this forward, is Coach Brian Williams. As a Christ believer, he knows how to allow God to speak to him through life experiences and knows that his life is not just all about him. He shows through this devotional that it is an important part of his life to impact the lives of others in a positive way.

As you read through this devotional you will receive great nuggets of knowledge and wisdom designed to help you grow in your walk with God. Don't just read the lessons, but be diligent enough to answer the Application Questions and then implement the Action Plan. With the aid of the Holy Spirit in doing so, you can't help but be successful. There are 52 chapters, one for each week of the year. How exciting it will be after you have completed that year to look back and see how far you have come on your victory road.

I have known Brian for about 20 years and know him as a great man of faith. I have watched him never waiver in his walk with God even when life hurled many difficult moments across his path. He knows how to press on toward the goal of heaven with God despite the life obstacles and challenges. I encourage you to allow the Lord to speak to you through the following pages. If I have ever been anything to Brian, it has been an encourager. Let him encourage you through his God inspired printed pages to develop your own great faith in the Lord and transform you into a person of victory. And remember this, God has a plan for your life and it's a *good* one.

– R. Dennis Bingham,
*Administrative & Missions Pastor,
Victorious Life Church*

In Loving Memory of Andrea Lopresti

Radiate Instead of Resolve

(Originally Written January, 2011)

When you are squeezed by life the deepest things inside of you come out!

Philippians 4:4 "Rejoice in the Lord always, again I say rejoice."

At the beginning of every year I set aside time with God to pray, journal and set goals. It is important to have a vision and plan then work toward those goals. However, at the beginning of 2011 I had a different perspective for the future realizing I missed a key part of life. This new perspective came from a phone conversation Claudia and I had on Christmas Day 2010 with a dear friend of ours from Tampa named Andrea. In April 2011 Andrea went home to Jesus and is now singing with the Angels in heaven. Below is a summary of Andrea's impact on me, which I wrote just after that Christmas conversation, and I hope it will also impact you.

Andrea is a gifted woman who constantly gives all she has to her husband, young sons and church family. When I lived in Tampa she "convinced" or should I say "corralled" me to be in theatrical productions she was directing (don't worry – I never sang). Her talent to organize and direct is amazing, and many Sunday mornings she blessed hundreds with her special talent of singing like an angel. She "radiates" Christ with her smile, words and presence.

Andrea's life took a big turn several months ago in late 2010. She was told by her Doctor that the pain she was feeling in her pelvis was cancer growing inside of her. Over the past few months she has had many doctor visits resulting in countless radiation and chemo treatments.

During our Christmas Day conversation with Andrea our plan was to wish her Merry Christmas and encourage her. Little did we know that God had another plan! When we got off the phone, we were both crying realizing that Andrea didn't just get radiation, she gave it. She radiated Christ in every area of her life! All she could talk about was how God was blessing her. She never brought up the pain or challenge. She saw it as blessing instead of a frustration that when she fell to the floor in the hospital she didn't also hit her head on a nearby ledge. She daily witnessed to nurses, doctors, and others around her at the hospital. Andrea's outlook wasn't bitter, it was better. People couldn't help but stop and talk with her and get their "radiation" treatment.

The doctors at one point found the cancer had spread so much in her brain that they couldn't count the number of cysts she had. They wondered how she was still alive and functioning. It's obvious God's plans for her supersede medical knowledge and He makes all the final decisions!

Visions, dreams and goals are great tools of God, but if we are not radiating Jesus Christ to others, we are missing the meaning of life. When He radiates through us, no matter what situation we find ourselves in, we are in God's plan. This year instead of a Goal, make it your daily life purpose to radiate Jesus – it will change your life and the lives of those around you.

1 EXCEPTIONAL

Live life through the power and strength of Jesus Christ!

2 Peter 1-5 "For this very reason, make every effort to add to your faith goodness; and to goodness, knowledge; and to knowledge, self-control; and to self-control, perseverance; and to perseverance, godliness; and to godliness, mutual affection; and to mutual affection, love."

Have you ever witnessed something so remarkable that it took your breath away? The first time I had this happen was one day in my late teens when I was standing at the top of Hoover Dam. This is one of the most amazing man-made structures on earth! It looked like an endless wall of concrete. I had the brief thought to rush down the side on a skateboard. I'm really glad I didn't do that.

This dam took more than five years to complete with the hard work of thousands of laborers. It now stands over 700 feet tall (twice the height of the Statue of Liberty) and in spots is over 600 feet thick (more than 2 football fields). The dam was built to hold back billions of gallons of water from the Colorado River to form Lake Mead.

Why is this dam so exceptional? Because it protects hundreds of thousands of lives while at the same time producing energy that sustains three states. The other exceptional thing is this impressive dam equals "self-control" in our personal lives. We have the power and authority through Jesus Christ to control how we live for him and what we let into our lives, but when we don't use that power wisely, it can be destructive!

If the Hoover Dam developed a tiny crack – even the size of a quarter – it would be overcome and destroyed by the water and so would thousands of people below it. In our lives, Satan tries to force cracks through our dam of self-control, which becomes sin. If a "sin crack" forms and is not immediately repaired (by turning to Jesus and asking forgiveness) it can lead to crumbled walls, destruction and loss of "power" in your life. This breach can also hurt many others around you.

To live in the fullness of Christ you must be serious about what you let into your mind, into your life, and into your habits. Weigh them against God's Word and commandments – day-by-day and moment-by-moment. Your life is meant to be and will be exceptional if you guard it. Your heart is the wellspring of life, so stay close to your Savior, keep your walls strong, and see the power that He will generate through your obedience.

Prayer:

"Lord Jesus, You are my all! Help me to desire only You! You are the answer to my every need, every hope and every longing. This world cannot fulfill, but can only leave me empty. You, Lord, are my fulfillment. You Lord are my all! Amen!"

Application Questions:

1. How important is it to live an "exceptional" life of walking with Jesus?

2. What are some of the spiritual disciplines you have in your life now?

3. How strong are the Christian disciplines you listed above?

4. In what areas of your life do you feel you have a "sin" crack?

5. What are new disciplines you need to add to your life to honor God and avoid cracks?

6. Who do you have in your life that can help you form these disciplines and keep them?

7. What's your prayer to Jesus to repent and commit to live an exceptional life with Him?

Action Plan:

Consider the area(s) in your life in which you struggle with temptation and sin. Some examples may be: selfish desires and attitudes, anger, jealousy, bitterness, fear, unbelieving, immoral thoughts, sexuality outside of marriage, lying, wanting someone else's things and lust. Write down what comes to mind. Next, ask God what you can do in each area to avoid the temptation or to avoid giving into it when it comes, then write your answer down. Finally, ask another brother or sister in Christ what walls they have in place to help them in these areas. As an example, if anger is your challenge, you may commit to memorize and recall scripture when feeling angry and your friend may have a tip for you, like taking a short walk to pray when anger starts to rise up.

A first tip on how to live a disciplined and wise life I heard many years ago from Billy Graham, is to read one chapter of Proverbs each day. Since there are 31 proverbs there is one for each day of the month to use.

2 FEAR NOT

The greatest maturity is to stay calm and trust in Christ – especially through difficulties

Mark 4:40 "He said to his disciples, 'Why are you so afraid? Do you still have no faith?'"

There is a story about a man who lived in a big city and provided for his family by pushing an apple cart. He worked hard and long hours. Customers would look forward to seeing this man every day on their way to work because he greeted everyone with a smile and was genuine. Sometimes he would give away food to a person who didn't have money. He always enjoyed what he did and earned enough to support his family.

Over time the man's son grew up and went off to Business College to learn about economics and finance while dad kept doing what he always did. One weekend his son came home to visit and help his dad at work. That evening the man's son told him about the struggling economy, the need to make bigger profits, and a necessity to cut down on giving. Dad listened. His prices went up and his giving went down – so did his income. Soon after, the man went out of business and had to hunt for a job to support his son at school and his struggling family.

How often do we listen to the voice of the world instead of God's voice? The world is convincing about its priorities and doubts! When we are walking close with God and focused on loving Him and others, the world looks different through His eyes. When we let the voice of the world and its worries ring in our ears, then God's still, small voice gets even smaller. We become like the man above who got away from caring for others and trusting God because of his newfound fear.

Jesus' disciples ended up in the same rut of worry even when Jesus was with them. Mark 4 reveals the disciples stuck in a boat in the middle of an intense storm. They set their focus on the storm they were in and the threat of death. It seems logical to us that they would be afraid – except that they forgot one thing. Jesus was with them.

They woke Jesus from sleeping probably hoping He would come up with an idea they hadn't yet thought about. He did. He spoke to the storm and quieted it. Then He rebuked His disciples saying, "Why did you fear, do you still have no faith?" Jesus says the same to you today. He has answers, solutions and miracles that have never even crossed your mind to cure your storm. He is not worried and He calls you to trust Him! Love others (by giving away your fruit – of the spirit) and follow God through whatever storms you may be facing.

Prayer:

"Lord Jesus, even Your disciples asked 'Who is this man that even the wind and the waves obey Him?' Lord, help me not to doubt You in any area of my life. Help me not to look with my eyes, but with my spirit at the deep truths of You. I believe in Your victory and know You have everything in the palm of Your hand – today and every day. I release all to You. Amen."

 **Application Questions:**

1. Would Jesus say to you today "what great faith you have" or "do you still have no faith"?

2. Do you believe God can handle anything that is going on in your life?

3. Are you pleasing God by trusting or sinning by worrying?

4. What scriptures do you daily claim as promises from God to overcome fear?

5. Who in your life can be a spiritual encouragement to you and how can they help?

6. When is the last time you offered help, support and prayer to someone else?

7. What do you want to say to Christ about living by faith and not by fear in your life?

 **Action Plan:**

Most of us worry, which in itself is a problem because God says it's a sin. The other problem is that most of our worries are about things that are out of our control, which wastes our time and can be paralyzing. Here are a couple simple actions steps that can make a huge difference in this area. First, take the three week challenge (to start a new habit) of every morning quoting and memorizing Joshua 1:9, which says, "Have I not commanded you? Be strong and courageous. Do not be afraid; do not be discouraged, for the LORD your God will be with you wherever you go." The other important action step is to keep a paper or small notebook with you and write a bullet point for each thing you find you're worrying about. Then categorize each worry either "in my control" or "out of my control". Work on a plan to improve the things in your control (a counselor or coach can help if needed) and things out of your control turn over to God.

3 USE YOUR GPS

Do you use your Holy Spirit GPS and more importantly, do you listen to it?

*Jeremiah 29:11 "'For I know the plans I have for you,' declares the L*ORD*, 'plans to prosper you and not to harm you, plans to give you hope and a future. Then you will call on me and come and pray to me, and I will listen to you. You will seek me and find me when you seek me with all your heart.'"*

I was recently on a business trip and was heading back to the airport. I was riding with a fellow employee who really didn't know where he was going. He handed me his phone, turned on the GPS, and said, "That little green dot is where we are, and the red one is where we are going. This will tell us how to get there". Awesome! It actually worked – at least when we listened to it. A few times we got impatient and went off course only to find a dead end, one-way street, or traffic jam. When we did actually follow the GPS, we ended up exactly at the right destination.

Global Positioning Systems for cars are very common in some places, but most of the world does not have them. However, every Christian does have an internal "Godly" Positioning System. This guidance is much better than any satellite man has created since it is a Holy Spirit driven connection and guides every area of our life – if we let Him.

I remember a joke from a famous elderly Preacher who said he won't use a GPS system because he won't have someone tell him where to go. Don't we all do that sometimes with God? We know what we want, and when He tries to direct us on the right path (His path), we choose to turn off His navigation and think we have a better path. Later we find we have caused ourselves more trouble and loss of time than if we had just stayed on course.

Think about this, if you were lost while driving and turned on your GPS, it would immediately show you where you are, where your destination is, and how to get there. If you follow it step by step, you arrive safely at your destination.

You may have lots of questions in your life right now. Turn on your Godly Positioning System and listen for God's "still small voice" (by praying, reading his Word, and being quiet). He will show you where you are (with Him), confirm your destination to His perfect place, and show you how to get there step by step. If you will listen and follow, He will steer you perfectly through life's turns, construction zones, and seemingly dead ends. He knows the way to your destination both here on earth and for eternity.

Prayer:

"Lord Jesus, lead me! Help me to be sensitive to Your spirit every day and every moment of my life. I want us to go together through all of life's journeys. Lead me, use me! Amen!"

 **Application Questions:**

1. Where do you get your direction for daily living and decisions?

2. How sensitive are you to listen for God's still small voice throughout the day?

3. Are you willing to follow God through every stop, turn and detour through life?

4. In the past, in what area of life have you gotten off course?

5. What is an area of life in which you are currently off God's path right now?

6. When God re-directs you, how quickly do you obey (and with what attitude)?

7. What can you do to tune into God's GPS each day and all through the day?

Action Plan:

Consider your day as a great adventure. You have an exciting destination with important stops along the way. The amazing thing is – you don't know the direction to go! You may have a basic plan, but you can't see the road of life ahead of you nor do you know how to navigate it other than by guessing. Now picture your life GPS box as the Bible and the voice as God's still small voice. Will you use your spiritual navigation system today, and how will you do it? You need to plan: 1) Where you will keep your "GPS" box handy all the time. Some ideas could be to keep a small one with you, put a Bible in your car or use a Bible app on your phone. 2) How to take time to listen for God's direction. Options could include a daily devotional time and scriptures posted in key places. 3) How you will stay committed to always follow God's direction. A Christian friend, coach or accountability partner can help with this

4 WHAT'S THE GOOD WORD?

How much are you "snacking" versus getting solid, filling daily "meals" from God's Word?

Hebrews 4:12 "For the word of God is alive and active. Sharper than any double-edged sword, it penetrates even to dividing soul and spirit, joints and marrow; it judges the thoughts and attitudes of the heart."

Back in the 1970's people would greet each other by saying "What's the Good Word?" – although I, of course, am not old enough to remember this. When someone would ask that question, the normal response would be something general or funny but never anything life changing. The good word wasn't really all that good; it was just words and updates.

We as Christians have another interpretation of the "good word" because it is really the "Good News". We know that the good news is the gospel of Jesus Christ and the salvation of the world through His blood shed. It is easy for us as Christians to know that truth, even share it with others, but lose the full impact of it in our daily lives.

There are so many great Bible teachers, story-tellers, and Christian encouragers you can read or listen to at any moment, that it is almost mind-boggling. These teachers do have an important part in our lives, and God tells us to learn from them. But don't fall into the trap of reading and listening to only those sources. The true source of all spiritual life is, and will always remain the same, the Holy Bible. As my father-in-law said, all learning materials we study from are good "snacks" but the very Word of God itself is the true meal each of us needs in order to live! God's Word is "Living and Breathing" – the very things we need!

I made a promise years ago to God that I would seek Him daily. The only two true ways I know to do that are through reading His Word and time in fervent prayer. There have been many days of battle just to try and keep this promise because Satan works hard to get us off track. But when you work at it, God will meet you and help you draw close to Him. He will never let you go! You need your life giving spiritual food to get through this day. Don't settle for less! Read or listen to God's Word daily!

Prayer:

"Lord Jesus, it is so easy to feel that I get my fill of You by going to church, attending a small group or even listening to your servants' teachings. Lord, I realize that nothing takes the place of You! Jesus, You are the word of God in the flesh and you said that we do not live by bread alone, but by every word that comes from You. I commit to daily "feeding" upon Your Word for my life – please help me do this. Amen."

Application Questions:

1. How much time are you spending in the actual Word of God daily?

2. Have you ever read (or listened to) the Bible all the way through?

3. When is the last time you got on your knees and humbled yourself before God in prayer?

4. What scriptures have you memorized and used on a daily basis for victory in life?

5. Can you live victoriously TODAY without ingesting God's "living and breathing" Word?

6. What percentage of your daily devotions is "snacking" versus "dining" with Christ?

7. Where is your daily place of refuge to pray and read God's Word?

Action Plan:

Pick a realistic time for you to spend just 10 minutes per day in God's Word. Commit to read (or listen to) one chapter of the Bible per day for the next 21 days. A couple of good places to start are Proverbs or John. Then decide if you will use a printed Bible, Bible software, Bible app or audio Bible to study from. Finally, jot down a couple things that impacted you from each chapter you read.

5 LIVING THE LIFE
Living a life that is partially following Christ is not following Christ

Revelation 21:7–8 "Those who are victorious will inherit all this, and I will be their God and they will be my children. 8 But the cowardly, the unbelieving, the vile, the murderers, the sexually immoral, those who practice magic arts, the idolaters and all liars—they will be consigned to the fiery lake of burning sulfur. This is the second death."

I recently saw one of my favorite preachers, Chuck Swindoll preaching on a Sunday morning TV broadcast. He stated that our country is sliding down a slippery slope and without a revival from God in our hearts, there is real trouble brewing. In all of his 74 years he has not seen such liberality, selfishness and tolerance of sin. Most people in the US say they believe in God, yet live no different than non-believers.

In a recent visit to Barnes and Noble, I was looking at a sales section of books for kids. The topics ranged from New Age to mystic. I opened a book named *Wands* just to see what kids are now reading. One section covered the history of wands and mysticism. Another focused on stars and horoscopes. The last section instructed a child "How to use a wand" and provided a real wand along with crystals to cast spells. Many adults see this as innocent, but it's actually condemned strongly by God as a major door opener to spiritual darkness and evil, as made clear to us in Revelation 21.

Chuck also said, "Whatever we tolerate, eventually we will become." We may not be a person who practices magic arts (or even allows our kids to), but if we don't reject it, we are accepting it. We may not be the person committing adultery with another, but if we watch things that promote it, we may be swayed to that action. We may not be the person committing acts of violence; yet continuing to accept it within the media may lead us to eventually act on it ourselves. If we bend the truth a little, this is still deceptive and sinful to God, and even if we are not the one telling foul jokes, but we laugh at them, it shows our acceptance.

We will never be perfect here on earth, but we are to live Holy Lives. Filling our minds and homes with unholy things can easily lead to a fall. "What you feed will grow and what you starve will die." We must stand up for what we believe and follow God at His Word. The first step in doing this is to not allow things we know that are sin into our own minds, lives or homes – even subtle things. Remember, by not rejecting sin you are supporting it.

Prayer:
"Lord, this is a difficult world we live in, as You said it would be. Please forgive me for accepting things that are not of You and help me to be Holy as You are Holy. Help me to know Your Word and follow it in every area of my life. Reveal to me the things I need to change in my life to better serve and glorify You. Help me to remove those habits, people or things that go against Your commands and perfect will. Thank You Lord Jesus. I love You! Amen."

 **Application Questions:**

1. What are you allowing into your mind, life and home that does not glorify God?

2. When do you find you "tolerate" things that you should be walking away from?

3. What do you need to change in your life to glorify God more?

4. If Jesus came to your house, what would you not want him to see that you do or have?

5. How can you put up safeguards against even allowing tolerance of sin?

6. Who is a Godly support in your life who can help you in making these changes?

7. What are you allowing your kids to fill their minds with?

Action Plan:

For one week keep a pencil and paper (or some other way to jot things down) handy, and record each time you notice you compromise your thinking, your speech, or your choices based on God's high calling for you. Look for trends and subtle weaknesses in your life that are holding you back from God's best. Make a commitment to God, yourself and an accountability partner that you will either stand your ground or remove yourself (based on God's truth) when this type of situation comes up again.

6 BEING A MAN

Men – don't forget who you are or what you were made to be and live it daily!

1 Timothy 1:7 "For God did not give us a spirit of timidity, but a spirit of power, love and self-discipline."

A little while back I was facing major struggles in all areas of my life. I will never forget going to our small group one Saturday evening and seeing this incredible replica of a Roman sword recently purchased by my brother-in-law. He is a black belt martial arts instructor and a very Godly man. He loves to be competitive and push himself, so it was no surprise to see him add another sword to his collection. This one, however, was fantastic and also marvelous because he bought it for me. I got choked up when he handed it to me along with an even more impressive sword – a new NIV Bible with commentary for men. If you are a man reading this, it is very important to pay attention – modern society hinges on you doing so. If you are a woman reading this, forward it on to the men God has put in your life to encourage.

A very well known lesbian sat and talked with a Christian woman who was describing her Godly husband and his holy attributes. The woman responded – "If I knew any guys like that, I would not have become gay!" Obviously, there are other issues in her life as well, but when men act and live as called to by God, it is not only respected by others – it is longed for in this world.

Right now there is a battle being waged, maybe stronger than ever, in history. The battle may one day result in a more physical one, but right now it is mental and spiritual in nature. Satan has strategically planted in society every conceivable way to pull a male away from God. There are not only temptations everywhere, but for the first time in history there is incredibly easy access to it (TV, movies, radio, billboards, easy travel, material goods, and the list goes on).

John Eldridge, in his book Wild at Heart talks about the three things at the core of every male. These are: an adventure to live, a beauty to save and a battle to fight. Guys, we were designed to be leaders and to set an example; to preserve, protect, and stand up for what God calls us to in our daily lives and in society. It is easy to become complacent, confused, and feel condemned, but God has called each of us to lead our families, lead society, and lead in whatever areas He puts us. We are to lead as led by Him. We must be great followers to be great leaders. We must be confident in who we are and whose we are to stand up for God's truth.

It is time to stand up and be counted! Your wife, your kids, your peers all look for this leadership in you. Are you willing to forsake all else and follow the Lord and to fight daily (spiritually) for what is true, holy and just in your own life and the world around?

Prayer:

"Lord Jesus, I am a man designed by You. Help me to follow You and to lead a life of holiness so that I may lead others around me – to You. Lead me, Lord, lead me. Amen."

Application Questions:

1. Are you the man God has called you to be in every area of your life right now?

2. What do you need to confess to God that has been a sin in your life?

3. What do you need to get rid of in your life to draw closer to God?

4. What do you need to add to your life (devotions, accountability) to draw closer to God?

5. What other Godly man can you talk to about these things and be accountable to?

6. Who can be a Godly male role model in your life?

7. Will you surrender all (on a daily basis) and take up your sword to follow Jesus?

Action Plan:

If you are a man reading this, it's time to take a stand. This week write out your commitment to God and to being the man He has called you to be. Spell it out in your own words. Write it from the heart then sign and date it. Don't take this lightly. It's time to take a stand. It's time to make a commitment to Him and to yourself. Share it with other close believers – you can even print them a copy. If you are a woman reading this, bring this idea up to the men who God puts on your heart. They may or may not agree to do this right away, but just by bringing it up you may get to talk deeply with the important men in your life. Keep praying for these men, we need it.

BEAUTIFUL

A woman who follows God is truly beautiful and makes things beautiful around her!

Proverbs 31:29 "Many women do noble things, but you surpass them all."

As a man, writing to men is easy, but writing to women can be more of a challenge. The first thing that came to my mind was the joke about the man who got the proverbial one wish from a genie. When he asked the genie to build him a road from California to Hawaii so he could drive there since he was afraid of flying, the genie said there was no way to do that. The time, labor and cost involved to build such an expensive structure would just be too much. He told the man to make another wish. This time the man asked to be able to understand women. The genie thought for a moment then responded, "Would you like that bridge to be two lanes or four?"

I realized I needed a women's perspective on being a Godly woman, so I asked my wife to help me. Claudia has always talked about the Proverbs 31 woman, but that chapter wasn't exactly what I was looking for since there are not many women these days dealing in wool and flax nor do they have servant girls to look over. Although there are many great things in that chapter, I asked Claudia how she would sum up a woman's role? Claudia immediately said submissiveness and surrender; then immediately another word came to my mind – "beauty".

The essence of a man is strength and power to achieve while the essence of a woman is beauty! This means true beauty not just physical beauty. Physical beauty is fleeting and only skin deep but true beauty is the glow and glory of God through all that a woman does. Unfortunately, in this world it can be difficult for a woman's true beauty to be seen because she has learned to conceal it due to stress, abuse, tough situations and even ungodly people around her.

I think of my wife's true beauty, besides her physical beauty. I see her true beauty when she is at peace and hearing from God, when she is giving of herself, when she accomplishes something God has called her to do, when she is creative at home, when she prays for me and others with a truly tender love, when she feels the love and protection of her husband, when she cries and feels others' hurts, when she submits her hopes and dreams to God, and when I see her nurturing children that come around her. These are just a few of the ways God's true beauty flows through her. If you are a woman who loves God, you are beautiful! Don't hide your beauty; Let it show, even in the hard times, by bringing God's love and caring to every situation.

Prayer:

"Lord Jesus, You are beautiful. Let Your beauty live through me for the world to see. Amen."

Application Questions:

1. Will you let the beauty of God's love and tenderness flow through you today?

2. If you are a woman, what holds you back from letting your true beauty shine?

3. If you are a man, how can you encourage the women around you appropriately?

4. What woman do you know that shows her true beauty all the days of her life?

5. If you are a woman, what do you need to change to start letting your true beauty out?

6. How important is it to you to love and support others unconditionally?

7. What scriptures can you stand on to let God live and shine through your life?

Action Plan:

If you are a woman reading this, you were made beautiful and still are. The stresses and trials of this world may have caused you to suppress it, but underneath it is who you are. Think about the times (which may be few) when your stress was low, your calendar was clear, and God shined His beauty through you. As you reflect on that time(s), write down what that felt like, what you were doing, and in what ways you were beautiful with God's love and joy. Now pray for God to reveal to you how to let Him shine through you again. Write down the areas of life, times and ways you can do this. You may need to make some changes and reprioritize your schedule to do this. If you are a man reading this, support the women in your life by helping them let their beauty shine. Pray for them; encourage them; and help provide them time and space to let the beauty of who God made them to be shine through. Start by picking a woman in your life you can do these things for (hint – if you are married it should definitely be your spouse).

THE CLOSING CEREMONY

Your Closing Ceremony will one day come!

Revelation 21:4–7 "He will wipe every tear from their eyes. There will be no more death or mourning or crying or pain, for the old order of things has passed away. He who was seated on the throne said, 'I am making everything new!' Then he said, 'Write this down, for these words are trustworthy and true.' He said to me: 'It is done. I am the Alpha and the Omega, the Beginning and the End. To the thirsty I will give water without cost from the spring of the water of life. Those who are victorious will inherit all this, and I will be their God and they will be my children.'"

Every four years the world is enthralled by the Summer Olympics. It's amazing to see all the world's best athletes come together in friendly competition. The closing ceremonies are especially moving as all the athletes who just competed against each other are in unity with thousands of fans in the stadium and millions watching around the world. Some athletes have medals, most do not, but they all are happy to have had the experience. They pushed it, they gave it their best – they made it to the Olympics. Soon we see the host country turn over the torch to the next host country, signifying their job is done. The country, the athletes, and even buildings all did their jobs.

You personally will have a closing ceremony at the time you leave this earth. You will either be here to see Christ's return, or it will simply be your time to go. You will transition from this world to the next. Because you are a Christian, all of heaven will attend your closing ceremony: the saints who went before you, your many loved ones, legions of angels, the elders of God's throne, Jesus Christ, the Holy Spirit, and the Father himself! They will all be cheering you on, applauding you for your faith and your love, and will be part of the celebration of your hope fulfilled! All of the hard work, dedication, blood, sweat and tears will be worth it.

You may feel you are in the middle of the battle right now – trying to "compete" in this world, trying to be victorious, trying to do God's will, but feeling like the finish line is miles away. The finish line may be right around the corner, or it may really be miles away, but keep your focus on your Father as He leads you to victory at the closing ceremony. You will make it! You will win the prize, and you will be cheered on by God and all of his creation.

If you did not have Christ as your Lord, your closing ceremony would be much different, but there is great news! Jesus died for you and has assured your place at that final ceremony if you accept him. Go to the section "Do you know Jesus?" at the front of this book to learn how.

Prayer:
"Lord Jesus, I want to see life in view of eternity. I realize I am only here on this earth for a short time, and I pray You help me make the most of every day. Help me live for You and be a witness for You today. Amen"

 **Application Questions:**

1. Do you realize all of heaven and Christ himself cheer you on and wait for your arrival?

2. How will you keep your eyes on Christ and listen to the Holy Spirit daily?

3. Are you giving it your all, realizing a crowd is watching your performance?

4. Do you realize some people you "battle" will be standing with you at the final ceremony?

5. Are you facing today's challenges in light of eternity?

6. Do you realize that all your medals, awards and everything else will be left here?

7. Are you living your life in order to bring glory to your "home nation"?

Action Plan:

Close your eyes for a few minutes to think about the last Olympic ceremony you watched. Reflect on that celebration you saw and how all the athletes rejoiced together, all the nations were in harmony, and millions around the world were in one accord. Now visualize the day when you will enter heaven, and realize, in your mind, that the Olympic celebration does not even compare. Many people around you today will be at that celebration, and some of them you might not even get along well with now. Think of three ways you will treat these foes lovingly on this earth (since you will be with them a long time in heaven). It does not mean you should be complacent on this earth or always giving in, but don't put this earth's priorities higher than eternal ones. Additionally, there are many others around you right now that have no ticket for the final celebration because they do not know Jesus. Pray for God to use you in their lives. Then schedule time to meet or talk with them this week just to build a relationship, then let God lead.

WHAT ARE YOU DOING TODAY?

To live by faith is to do what you say you believe – every day!

Romans 14:23 "Anything not done in faith is sin."

The Bible is filled with a key word that is the very beginning and core to our walk with God. That word is "Faith", which really means "belief". Why is this important? Because without it, we cannot please God! Every Christian says they have faith, but faith is both a noun and a verb (based on the word for faith used in the Bible). You cannot have faith by just believing something in your mind, you have it by acting upon that which you say you believe.

God may have given you great dreams and visions for your life, but you have a part to play in making them happen. You have to do what God shows you to do. It may be a schedule change, a job change, a phone call, an apology to make, or even a big first step into a new adventure. The point is that you must listen to God, believe what you hear, then do what He is calling you to do.

The polar opposite to faith is a four-letter word that we don't like to hear – fear. Joyce Meyers said there really aren't various types of fears (i.e. fear of success, fear of failure, fear of people, etc.). She believes there is really only the fear of one thing – pain. This may come in the form of physical pain, emotional pain, relational pain, etc. We all want to move away from pain into comfort. Unfortunately that fear of pain is the exact opposite of the faith God calls us to. Fear can paralyze even Christians into not doing anything.

There was a movie out years ago called Simon Birch. It was about a misfit boy who always seemed to be getting into trouble, but in his heart knew he had a purpose. Not to give away the plot, but there came a point when Simon had to risk his life to save the other kids. He was the only one who could do it because of his size. He moved in faith despite the fear because there was a bigger purpose for him to achieve. That same principle holds true for us. Satan tries to convince us to play it safe, but the only way to overcome fear is to trust in God, then act on faith.

No matter how contradictory or opposite God's next steps may seem to you (compared to what you desire), true faith is trusting that God has your perfect path in hand. Imagine what would happen if all Christians walked by faith instead of fear. Imagine that one of those Christians is you – starting right now. Remember, anything not done in faith is sin.

Prayer:

"Lord Jesus, there is absolutely nothing too big for You! I believe that! I do have faith in You, but just as the man said to You in scripture, I also ask of You – Lord 'increase my faith'. Help me not to live a shallow life, but instead a full life that is based on faith and reflected in what I think, and what I do. Help me not to fear pain, but instead focus on You and Your promise of victory in my life. Amen."

Application Questions:

1. Have you surrendered everything in your life to Jesus Christ?

2. How much time are you spending with Jesus on a daily basis?

3. Are you praying, reading the Bible, and taking time to listen during your daily devotions?

4. What is Jesus calling you to do?

5. What are you going to do today to walk by faith into what God has shown you?

6. Who is a person strong in faith whom you can talk to and confide in?

7. What would you like to say to Jesus right now?

Action Plan:

How would you rate your level of faith in the areas of hearing and trusting in God? Consider that a 1 would be that you don't really believe in Christ, you don't seek Him for your answers nor do you hear His directions, and a 10 means you daily (and throughout the day) listen for God's direction and follow up every time. If you're at a 10, congratulations – there are not many people who consistently live at that level. If you rank yourself below a 10, think about what is holding you back from living life at a deeper level of faith in Christ. Remember, fear is not from God. So what are the next steps you can take in your life to walk by faith this week?

10 TAKE INVENTORY

You cannot manage what you do not measure.

Colossians 3:23–25 "Whatever you do, work at it with all your heart, as working for the Lord, not for human masters, since you know that you will receive an inheritance from the Lord as a reward. It is the Lord Christ you are serving. Anyone who does wrong will be repaid for their wrongs, and there is no favoritism."

Life can get busy and become a blur which can cause us to lose our sense of where we are within God's plan for us. It is important as Christ followers to slow down and take inventory of our lives to make sure we are walking with Him and heading in the right direction. We are called not only to learn about how to manage our lives the way God wants us to, but also to do what He asks. To have God's blessing in all areas of our lives, we must dedicate all those areas to Him.

A powerful way to know if your whole life is glorifying God is to take an inventory of each area periodically. The best time to do this is during your devotional time when you are already spending time with God in prayer and Bible reading. Just set aside some additional time every three or six months to review your life and direction and ask God what He wants you to focus on.

Some of the key areas to review through prayer are: spiritual, mental, relational, financial, health, career, ministry, time, and recreation. It is amazing how different areas of our lives can be so off track according to what God wants because we don't see the forest for the trees. Think of it this way: If all areas of your life are balanced but one is off, your health for example, and God wants you to build a relationship with someone or work in a ministry you may not be able to because you don't have energy to do it. You can't fulfill God's bigger purpose, which is to love Him and to love others.

We are responsible to live our lives by doing what the Bible says: to glorify God with all areas. We are called to be like Jesus who was the most balanced person to ever walk the earth. There are lots of scriptures that apply to different areas of our lives. As you study God's Word during your devotional time, look to see what He has to say about these areas and how to live them according to His will. If you do your part to honor God's calling and direction, He will fulfill every good purpose of yours and every act prompted by your faith.

Prayer:

"Lord, help me to live every day according to Your will. I pray that You would help me to take responsibility for all the areas of my life so that I may glorify You in all I think, say and do. Help me also realize those things that I can't control so that I can lift them up to You in faith knowing that You will work all things together for good. In the name of Jesus Christ, I pray. Amen."

 **Application Questions:**

1. How is your relationship with Christ and are you letting Him direct your life?

2. How well do you keep your mind on God and the things he would have you do?

3. How pleasing to God are your relationships with family, friends, coworkers, etc?

4. How well do you manage not only money but all things for God's purposes?

5. How well do you take care of your physical body (the temple of the Holy Spirit)?

6. Are you in or pursuing the kind of vocation in which God can best use your gifts?

7. Are you productive in using your time to the purposes that God wants you to?

 **Action Plan:**

Pick a day over the next week to set aside extra time during your daily devotions to look at these key areas of your life. Take this time to ask God to reveal where you are doing well and where you are struggling. You can do this by listing the key areas (such as spiritual, mental, relational, financial, health, career, ministry, time, recreation, attitude, etc.). Find a scripture that applies to them then rank each area 1–10 according to how well you're doing in that area. For any area under 7, list the actions you will take to improve it, and decide when you will start working on it. If you would like help go to www.coachbrianwilliams.com for some free tools to help you with this.

11 YOUR LIFE ADVENTURE

Life will either be an exciting adventure or a real drudgery – the choice is up to you.

Hebrews 11:1 "Faith is being sure of what you hope for and certain of what you do not see."

In 2004 an Olympic gold medal was placed around the neck of an Argentinean basketball player who lost his mother and wife in a car accident in little more than a year before in June, 2003. The exact same day one year later, just weeks before the Olympics he also lost his father. He never gave up but kept his eye on the prize. Through the major challenges and obstacles he moved forward towards his purpose until standing on the podium that day.

We were not put on this earth to suffer for 90 years then die. We were meant to live here on earth, then for eternity to be with Jesus. Life is filled with disappointments, struggles, and let downs. How you respond to them determines if you make your future better or worse. I believe this truth was summed up by a friend of mine who said, after the tragic death of a God- loving 15 year old from his church, "The real tragedy of life is not death. The real tragedy in life is not living."

Life is an incredible journey if we live it that way! This is especially true if you follow Jesus Christ! Many non-Christians consider the Christian life to be boring. If you look at it based on how many "proclaiming" Christians live it – it is! However, the true Christian life is not and cannot be boring because it is based solely on faith. When you live by faith, make decisions on faith, and stake your future completely on your faith in Jesus Christ, you can't possibly be bored.

Consider that Jesus lived a full life until the day He died. Jesus also lived every day through faith. They are one in the same – real faith equals real life. The way to live a truly abundant life is by really listening for God's voice and following, no matter what He leads you to do. He may call you to witness or pray for someone you never met. He may lead you to an area out of your comfort zone. God may give you a vision that will require effort, perseverance, and dependence on Him. When you are stretched by God and follow in faith, you will be living life to its fullest.

Christ came so that we may have life and have it abundantly. The question is – do you have abundant life? It doesn't mean everything is rosy and happy all the time. Nor does it mean you have everything you want in life. It does mean there is purpose, joy, peace, fulfillment, and passion in your life as you walk day by day in faith with Jesus.

Prayer:

"Lord Jesus, You are my Lord and my King. You are my savior; my everything. I trust my life to You and ask You to help me to live life to its fullest, just as You did when You walked here in human flesh. I don't want to live a mediocre life, but one that totally trusts in You and is filled with joy, peace and the excitement of another day. As I face struggles, help me to have the right attitude and please help me also to encourage others to do the same. Amen."

Application Questions:

1. Do you have the Joy of the Lord at the core of your being?

2. Do you have peace in whatever situation(s) you are going through?

3. Are you living life to its fullest and making it an exciting adventure, or is it a drudgery?

4. What have you been afraid to step out in faith on in your life?

5. What is your biggest fear?

6. Do you believe if Jesus calls you to it, He will empower you to do it?

7. How will you face your fear through the power of Jesus and move forward in faith today?

Action Plan:

There is a powerful quote that says "You can't just get rid of a bad habit, you have to replace it with a good one." If you have been living your life proclaiming to be a believer yet not fully walking in faith, you have a bad habit. That habit may be that you don't listen to God or that you know what he is calling you to do but you don't obey because of fear or even just because you want your own way. What is the way you really want to live your life? Think of the new responses and habits you need to put into your life to truly live by faith. Share these changes you are making with a friend. Pray for God's power and guidance, then make a three week commitment to change your habit and live by faith.

12 LIFE'S HURRICANES

Life's hurricanes will come but you will be secure on the rock

Matthew 7:25 "The rain came down, the streams rose, and the winds blew and beat against that house; yet it did not fall, because it had its foundation on the rock."

Some years back when Claudia and I lived in Tampa, Florida, we experienced the effects of two major hurricanes within a six-week period. Thankfully we were not in the direct path of the hurricanes, and we were spared major losses. However, we did experience some effects of the storms, including high gusty winds, loads of rain, and loss of "important" life conveniences – like phones and electricity. The biggest impact though, was our anxiousness while the hurricanes were approaching, as both Charlie and Ivan were forecasted to be direct hits.

After the first two hurricanes, I finally learned my lesson. When I knew the third one was approaching, I found myself waiting in line at the local Home Depot at 5 a.m. to purchase plywood to protect our home. Apparently everyone else learns by desperate experiences also, because I was joined in line by over 100 of our neighbors. We took other precautions too, like turning up the refrigerator and freezer, filling our bathtubs with water, and purchasing lots of supplies. We even had an evacuation plan ready to leave for Georgia if the course of Ivan did not change. Thankfully that highly destructive hurricane did not hit our area, but we still got some of its effects.

We all experience the "hurricanes" of life. These are the destructive, uncontrollable situations that are much bigger than we are. Some of them hit us head on while others may miss us but still have an impact in some way. If you don't prepare, you can be caught off guard and end up with really bad results. God gives us ways to face these hurricanes: through prayer, by being watchful and by completely trusting in Him.

We must be spiritually strong and ready for life's storms by standing on God's Word. This comes through preparing ourselves by putting on the armor of God just like we put plywood on the house. Listening to truth about the situation through prayer is even more important than listening to the weather reports. You should have a hurricane type emergency plan for your everyday living. These are some of the examples of what to include in your day to day plan: know what route to take in your life, let others know your situation, and ask others to be praying for you.

Prayer:

"Lord Jesus, You are the God of all. Nothing surprises You and nothing is bigger than You. I pray for Your guidance and protection. Help me to trust in You to avoid all the storms that I should not go through and to be prepared for those on my course. I pray that through these life challenges You strengthen my walk with You, the confidence in myself and my witness to others. I love You and trust in You for all things. Amen."

Application Questions:

1. What are some hurricanes you have been through in life?

2. How do you see that God was faithful to you through those hurricanes?

3. How did you weather the past storms in life?

4. What hurricanes are you now facing?

5. How firmly do you feel you are fastened to the rock of Christ and His promises?

6. Are you closely listening for God's guidance day-by-day and moment-by-moment?

7. How do you prepare for today's challenges and life's hurricanes?

Action Plan:

Think about the most recent "life hurricane" you faced or are facing now. Consider the things that were strong in your life and helped you through. Write those down in your journal, then put a check mark next to each of those areas that is still strong in your life today. Recognize the areas that have no check mark and may be slipping and the areas that you need to strengthen. Next, think of what things were not in place before that hurricane and would have been a tremendous help in surviving the storm and write them down. Some of these areas may include: knowing and standing on God's Word, putting on the armor of God daily, (see Ephesians 6:10–18), listening to truth about the situation from God through prayer, knowing exit routes with a biblical plan, and having support from others who know your situation and how to pray for you. Now consider the areas listed and take them one by one and begin putting these into your life over the next weeks and months. Think of someone (or have a coach) to help you strategize and hold you accountable as you do this.

13 YOUR PERSONAL ECONOMY

The borrower is servant to the lender so who is your master – hopefully not "master" card!

Proverbs 22:7 "The rich rule over the poor; And the borrower is servant to the lender."

How are you doing financially right now? It is quite apparent that our U.S. economy and the world economy are struggling to even survive. The situation reminds me of an e-mail I sent to a friend in September of 2008 – when there were only talks about the first bailout program the government was considering. My friend had asked me my thoughts on the economy, and I wrote him a four-paragraph e-mail explaining what I saw happening. Here is a portion of that e-mail.

"In my opinion, no one, including our government, in this country is getting to the root of our economic problem, which is living in debt (slavery), Since God says the borrower is servant to the lender, we (the people) have become servants to all the financial institutions because of our cars, homes, credit cards, etc. that now control us and require us to be "slaves" to our work, not servants of God. An even bigger problem is that our government and most of our major institutions are now slaves to the rest of the world (which includes volatile countries) because we have sold out our assets and debt instruments that we (the people) are obligated to pay.

Therefore, the United States is mainly now a servant to those who control the financial institutions – which, for the most part, are foreign companies and foreign governments. The whole mindset of this country has unfortunately turned to greed and impatience, and has caused an American nightmare. Without some fundamental shifts, I think we will see some major reckoning from God until we get back to His principles. We, as a country, need to humble ourselves and ask for His guidance, then act on His principles to get us out of our national and personal debt."

Ultimately everything in the world belongs to God – every asset, every home, every dollar, etc. Psalm 50:10–15 says everything in the world is His. It also says "Sacrifice thank offerings to God, fulfill your vows to the Most High, and call upon me in the day of trouble; I will deliver you, and you will honor me." Our answer is very simple – recognize that God owns it all and follow His plan for managing finances. It starts with a biblical principle that sounds crazy to the world, which is tithing. Tithing is giving God the first 10% of your income in faith and standing on His promise that you cannot out give Him. He will provide for you. If we put God first in our country and personal finances, we will be restored. Until we decide to live that way – God have mercy on us!

Prayer:

"Lord Jesus, all I want is You! I trust in You to supply all my needs. Here's my life, here are my belongings, and here is my money. I trust in You to provide for my family and me. Amen"

Application Questions:

1. Are you more focused on God or the news when it comes to your financial future?

2. Is there anything in your life that is more important to you than God?

3. How much are you praying for the leaders and the revival of this country?

4. What principals do you use to manage your personal finances?

5. Are you servant to anyone other than God because of debt?

6. What percent of your income do you give back to God?

7. Do you pray for your finances?

Action Plan:

This Action Plan is simple yet not easy if you don't already tithe. Tithing is giving God your "first fruits" or first earnings. My parents taught me how to do this from a young age and God always provided for my family every day of every year. Things were not always how we wanted them to be, but we always had a roof over our heads, clothes for our bodies, food on our plates, and adequate transportation. The goal is to give back to God (through your church) 10% of your income. That may be tough to immediately start with, so pray about it. Definitely start with something – immediately. Determine what percent you will start giving and if you absolutely can't start with 10%, start with what you can. Consider increasing by 1% each month until you get to 10%. There are lots of other things important to do financially (budgeting, etc.), but this is the first priority and a promise from God. You may ask if you should give off your Gross or Net income. You can pray about that too. Personally, we give based on gross income.

14 GET OUT OF YOUR BOAT

What is your boat – and what is your water?

Matthew 14:22–25 "Immediately Jesus made the disciples get into the boat and go on ahead of him to the other side, while he dismissed the crowd. After he had dismissed them, he went up on a mountainside by himself to pray. Later that night, he was there alone, and the boat was already a considerable distance from land, buffeted by the waves because the wind was against it. Shortly before dawn Jesus went out to them, walking on the lake."

I am sure you have heard people say that they don't walk on water, meaning they are not perfect or they are not Jesus. Even more amusing is when these same people say there is only one person that has ever walked on water, and it's not them. Although there is much truth to the point that it is a miracle to walk on water (in case you haven't tried it lately), it is not true that only Jesus has done it!

In Matthew 14, Jesus sent his disciples on ahead of him by boat to their destination. He, on the other hand, decided to catch up with them in a very unusual way – He walked out to them on the water. Needless to say – the disciples were "freaked out" (not the exact Hebrew translation). Once Peter knew who it was, he asked Jesus to command him to come to Him, which Jesus did. The other incredible miracle is that Peter also walked on water – for a short time!

Peter originally would not get out of his place of safety, the boat, on his own (very wise). He waited until Jesus called him to come out of the boat first (very wise). Peter stepped out of his comfort into the fear of the unknown by trusting in Jesus (very wise). Peter kept his eyes on Jesus and walked toward him on the water (very wise). Peter then took his eyes off Jesus and put them on the "boisterous" wind and began to sink because of fear (not so smart).

Even though Peter fell, Jesus caught him and said, "You of little faith, why did you doubt?" That tells me Peter would have stayed on top of the water if he had kept his eyes on Jesus. I give Peter credit since he was the only one who had the courage to get out of the boat. Would you have? Will you now?

As a disciple walking with Jesus, nothing was normal – everything was extraordinary and miraculous. We are His disciples today and should still expect the same from Him now. Instead of staying in your comfortable "boat", ask Him to call you out. Take the step of faith, and then keep your eyes on Him – expecting miracles.

Prayer:

"Lord Jesus, I read about You and all the miraculous things You did through those who loved You. You said You would do even greater things now than You did centuries ago. Help me not to doubt but to believe. Call me out of my boat to walk on water with you to experience the miraculous. Amen!"

Application Questions:

1. What boat of comfort do you find yourself in today?

2. What is the water outside your boat that scares you just to think of stepping onto it?

3. When is the last time you asked Jesus to call you out of the boat?

4. Did you follow Jesus the last time He called you out of the boat?

5. How hard is it for you to keep your eyes on Jesus?

6. Where are you hearing Jesus calling you out to now?

7. Will you live to hear "why did you doubt" or "well done good and faithful servant"?

Action Plan:

Write down in your journal or planner the area God is showing you to get out of the boat. Next, write down how you feel about taking that step of faith (both positives and negatives) then pray and ask Jesus to confirm that He wants you to take this step of faith, just as Peter did. Also Pray through each of the negatives on your list and ask God to speak to you about them. Write down what he shows you. If this is from Christ, He will not only confirm in your spirit (through others, His word, circumstances, etc.) that He is calling you to this step of faith, but He will speak to you about the obstacles as well. Finally, set a specific time to step out of the boat and recruit someone to pray for and encourage you to keep your eyes on Jesus and not the storm.

15

FEAR NOT!

God does not suggest we trust in Him for everything – our Father expects it

*Isaiah 41:13 "For I am the L*ORD *your God who takes hold of your right hand and says to you, Do not fear; I will help you."*

It is so easy to read the word of God and believe it intellectually. It's even quite easy to encourage people around you by quoting scripture and supporting them in prayer, but when you yourself are in a valley, everything looks completely different. The mountains seem higher, the path has been erased, and the nights are dark with unfamiliar sounds. It's amazing how a month, a week, or even a day can change so quickly: you can go from helping others that are "in the valley" to now being in one yourself.

We will all experience valleys in life. When we are in them we don't think we should be there. We think, "Isn't it obvious God's children should never be in the valley but always on the mountain top?" If you have been living for Christ for long, you may have thought this, but Christ promised we would have trials and tribulations. He was not exempt from them and neither are we! It is not hard to theologically explain why we go through these valleys. More important though is to know we will go through them, and God will use those times for a great purpose.

So if we know we are going to face these challenges, how should we do it? The answer is "with Jesus"! He tells us to face these challenges without fear. How can we really do that since there seems to be so many good reasons for us to worry, fear, and doubt? The key is what we focus on. If Christ just said "Fear Not" (Sounds like a good tee shirt logo), we would have big problems because there is no power behind it. But then He says, "For I am with you!"

The Lord and maker of the universe went through more than you and I could ever imagine, all while living a sinless life. He is with you – right now! Right now Jesus sees you, hears you, and knows your struggles. Think about that for a moment. Wherever you are, whatever you are doing, and whatever you are going through – Jesus Christ, Lord of the universe, is with you. Turn your thoughts on Him since He already has the path for you to walk. Just like the soldiers who have night vision and can see things in the dark even though you can't, Jesus sees the path through your darkness. Don't focus on what your mind thinks it perceives; focus on Him and you will soon realize all fear, worry, and doubt have faded away.

Prayer:

"Lord Jesus, help me not to just be a hearer of Your word but also a doer of it. Your Word tells us to fear not. I ask for You to put peace and power in my life right now and for this day because I know You are with me. Let Your perfect love drive out any fear that Satan tries to put in my mind and renew a right spirit within me. Amen."

Application Questions:

1. How can you realize deeply that Christ is with you right now?

2. What do you find yourself focused on most of the time, fear or Jesus?

3. Do you have 4 or 5 scripture promises from God that you consistently claim for your life?

4. What fears do you need to give over to God?

5. Have you asked Jesus to increase your faith?

6. When is the last time you moved against your fear by taking a step of faith?

7. Who in your life can stand with you in faith (and you with them) to follow Christ?

Action Plan:

Think of at least three difficult times God has brought you through. How did He do it? Some of His rescues may have even been miraculous, and it's important to realize "nothing is impossible with God." Now apply that truth to your current or next challenge by realizing God is and will always be faithful. Find at least three scriptures that direct your focus to God and not your problem, then quote them daily. A couple examples to consider are Joshua 1:9 and Isaiah 26:2. Finally, ask God to increase your faith since He is the giver of faith, and to give you a clear vision of Him for the day.

16 STAYING YOUNG

It is important to have the wisdom of an adult but the faith of a child.

Luke 18:16 "But Jesus called the children to him and said, 'Let the little children come to me, and do not hinder them, for the kingdom of God belongs to such as these. Truly I tell you, anyone who will not receive the kingdom of God like a little child will never enter it.'"

It seems the older we get the more skeptical we become. As we get "burned" by situations in life we tend to build high walls and to get very cautious about getting hurt again. Contrast that to a child who doesn't know any better and instinctively trusts everyone. There seem to be stages in life we go through that teach us to be cautious and not trust, however, we can take this to an extreme.

When it comes to walking with God, Jesus said we are to have faith like a child! That seems harder to do the older we get. At five years old, if you feel a tug on your heart to give someone your sandwich, you will do it immediately. At 30 or 40 years old most people won't do it. As we grow older it is important to have the wisdom of an adult but the faith of a child.

There are three voices you hear in your mind. One is yours, the other is Satan's and the most important is God's still, small voice. The key to having faith like a child is to know where the direction is coming from. Learn to exercise wisdom to understand what you are hearing to know when it's not from God and where the voice is coming from through prayer and reading the Bible. If it's from God – believe it, act on it and trust in God for the outcome.

Think about a person in your life that you are very close to such as a parent, sibling, spouse, or friend. If that person called you on the phone and you didn't have caller ID, you would still immediately recognize his or her voice. The longer and closer you walk with God, the easier it will be to recognize His voice.

The bigger the situation or decision the more emotional it is. This is Satan's playground for confusion. It is very important to seek God through these decision-making times. A good way to do this is to give it to God and put the situation to the back of your mind. Decide not to even think about for days or even weeks. If the idea is from you or Satan, the pull to do it will go away on its own. If the voice is God's, it will get stronger and tug at your heart as you pray for God's will. When you're confident it's God, have faith like a child and follow His call!!!

Prayer:

"Lord Jesus, help me have faith like a child – because I am (Your child). Help me also to have wisdom to know Your voice versus my own or Satan's. When I sense it is You, I will walk by faith and do what You call me to do. Help me to be like the men and women I read about in the Bible who walked with You, knew Your voice and did amazing things as led by Your Holy Spirit. Amen!"

 **Application Questions:**

1. How childlike is your faith?

2. How much time do you take searching out God's will for big decisions in your life?

3. Will you set aside your big decisions in order to pray for God to tug at your heart if it's Him?

4. How willing are you to let an idea go once you realize it's not God directed?

5. Who do you know that walks through life with faith like a child?

6. Do you seek out the still small voice compared to the loud and exciting ones of life?

7. Why is it important for you to hear God's voice?

 **Action Plan:**

Think about what you used to dream about as a kid. Remember "what you wanted to be when you grew up." Think about the profession you wanted to have, the adventures you thought would be exciting, or the social times with others (maybe tea parties or marriage ceremonies for the women). Regardless of where your life is now, it is still important to dream and to be inspired by God. What stirs your heart now when you think through your child eyes again? Regardless of your age, become a child in your faith by asking God to give you dreams and visions of the things He has planned for you, then write them down. Ask Him to show you how to begin to put some or all of this into your life. Trust God and walk in the excitement and faith of life.

17 PERSONAL DEVELOPMENT
Let God do His part and you do yours

Proverbs 14:12 "There is a way that appears to be right, but in the end it leads to death."

I have spent many years coaching others in all types of life situations, including spiritual, financial, relationships, business, and health. I frequently am asked where the separation is between trusting in God to take care of everything versus working on things ourselves using our strength or ambition. In other words – who really has responsibility? Great question!

The answer lies in our relationship with our Heavenly Father. He is our Dad and we are his children. He has promised us many things in this life and in the life to come (if we have accepted Jesus as our Savior). However, we are not to put our lives on cruise control to sit back and just let God do everything. We were each put here for a reason and are given work to do.

In the world of motivational speaking and self-improvement, there is a lot of truth to what is taught. For instance: we are wired for accomplishment, there are "energy" levels in creation, it really does matter what you think and what your attitude is. Many of these things are principles God has set up since the beginning of time. Unfortunately, most of these motivators fall short by teaching that you should go after whatever your heart desires. They leave out the most important point of life – God is relational and has a good and perfect will for your life, and He will lead you.

Again, Matthew 16:26 asks, "What good will it be for a man if he gains the whole world, yet forfeits his soul?" All the principles God created in the world are good, but they are not an end in themselves. You could use all the great principles of investing, time management, and goal setting, yet be on your own path and not God's. You could literally obey every biblical principle in life yet not accept Jesus as Lord, and still miss your calling on this earth and eternity in heaven.

The most fulfilling life you can have is one that is surrendered to God through Christ, (knowing why you were created and living out that purpose). As Christians, we are responsible to seek Christ and He is responsible to lead us. As we follow and give everything our best effort He ensures us the outcome is in His hands. When you are spending time with God, trusting Him, loving Him, following Him, and living by His principles of truth in this world, then you are truly successful – no matter what the outcome is!!!

Prayer:
"Lord Jesus, help me to first love You. Show me Your will and Your way and let me settle for nothing less in my life. Whatever course You take me on, let me not look at the results I see to judge my true success, but instead follow You with my life and leave the results to You. I desire to please You through passion and conviction to pursue and accomplish Your purpose. Amen."

Application Questions:

1. How much do you focus on doing things "right" versus listening to God?

2. Are you on God's chosen path for you right now?

3. If you are not on His path, what do you need to do to get on it?

4. Are you living based on His principles regarding your time, money, and talent?

5. Are your goals coming from God or your own motivations?

6. Have you surrendered everything to God?

7. What do you need to know from God to confirm you are on His path?

Action Plan:

There are four parts to fully achieving this action plan. The first is to ask yourself, "Am I seeking God's will in every area of my life?" If you cannot answer "yes" to this question, what do you need to do or surrender in order to do this? Until you are seeking God's purpose in every area, the next steps won't matter. Once you are seeking Him, pay attention in order to sense and hear His direction (this is good to capture somewhere in writing to remind you). Now, are you walking in obedience to what He shows you? If not, consider what you need to change to come in line with His direction, and then make those changes. Once you are seeking Him in all areas, hearing His direction, and following with your best effort – have peace! Jesus is responsible for the outcome! Regardless of what happens, if you are doing your part, He is faithful. He will lead you; He will take care of you!

18 DO THE LAST THING GOD SHOWED YOU!

Do the last thing God showed you until He opens the door or shows you something different.

Exodus 14:13 "Moses answered the people, 'Do not be afraid. Stand firm and you will see the deliverance the LORD will bring you today.'"

There are times in life when it seems we have clear directives from God about what to do and how to handle a situation. However, there are other times we don't have such incredible clarity and insight into God's plan for our daily living. Why is that? Especially when Ephesians 5:17 tells us "do not be foolish, but know what the Lord's will is." God would not tell us to know His will if there wasn't a way for Him to reveal it to us!

Think back to some of the times when you clearly felt God leading you in something, and you followed. How did He show you His plan? Sometimes it's through His Word; sometimes it's through other people, other times through prayer or even a confirmation of your prayer. God can use many ways to reveal His will. Always know that when it's Him speaking to you, that still small voice inside of you will give peace to your spirit.

There are many other times when God seems quiet. What do we do then? Consider Job. He asked God for an answer for quite some time before he heard any response. Daniel had to fast over 20 days for His answer because the angel that was sent to deliver God's message was held up by Satan in the heavenly realms. There could be many reasons you don't get your answer to prayer right away, but in these times you must remain faithful.

Consider the parable of the seed that fell on the ground. The first seed fell on the ground and the birds ate it, which symbolizes hearing God but doubting His word and not following in faith. The second seed fell where there was little soil, so it sprouted fast then was burned up, which symbolizes hearing God's word and believing for a short while, until trials come, then losing faith. The third fell among thorns and was choked out, which symbolizes the worries and negative impressions of this world. However, the last fell on good soil that produced a huge crop. That good soil is your faith!

When God gives you a seed (or Word), you must stand on the promise of that word and not let it get eaten, burned up or choked out. You must persevere and believe! Trust God and stay the course until he opens the door or shows you a change in direction. When the Egyptian army cornered the nation of Israel at the Red Sea, God led Moses to say to the Israelites, "Stand firm and you will see the deliverance the Lord Has for you." Sometimes that's true for your walk too!

Prayer:

"Speak to me Lord for Your child is here, listening. Speak to me Lord for Your child is here, waiting on You. Unveil my eyes and let me see You. Unveil my heart and let me know You – Father." – From "Speak to me" by Rebecca St. James

 **Application Questions:**

1. How often do you seek to hear Christ speak to you?

2. How intently do you listen for Him?

3. How do you know when God is talking to you?

4. What is the last thing God showed you to do?

5. How faithful have you been to following it?

6. What kind of attitude do you have while waiting for God to show you the next step?

7. Would Jesus say to you "well done good and faithful servant" at the end of each day?

Action Plan:

This will be helpful if there is an area in your life that you feel stuck in. Maybe you've been in that one place for a long time. Think of that area and about when the last time was that you really prayed to God about it and asked Him to reveal His will to you and to show you the next steps. If it has been a while since you have done this, start there. Give it some time of consistent prayer – at least a few days. An amazing way to communicate with God is during your devotional time. Write down your question to God, and many times He will pop the answer into your mind. Make sure to write that down as well. For some reason writing down your thoughts helps give you clarity from God. If you have been doing this and still get no answer, think back to the last thing God showed you about this area of life, and stay faithful to that until He reveals His next steps. Obviously, keep the area in prayer, but don't dwell on it – wait for God's timing.

19

TRUSTING JESUS

Your faith in God only shows true when you're tested beyond your own capabilities.

Romans 8:28–30 "And we know that in all things God works for the good of those who love him, who have been called according to his purpose. For those God foreknew he also predestined to be conformed to the image of his Son, that he might be the firstborn among many brothers and sisters. And those he predestined, he also called; those he called, he also justified; those he justified, he also glorified."

Have you ever had Christ almost shout at you through what you saw and heard until you finally got the point? I remember a few years back Claudia and I had this experience as a major theme kept coming at us all day: during our morning devotional, on the radio during our drive to church, on the marquee in front of a church on our way, in our own church service, and even from Claudia's mom later that day. God kept telling us through every source he could – "Be patient" and "wait on the Lord".

Since we were in the middle of some trials in our lives, this was the last thing we really wanted to hear. Our own minds want to hear about the swiftness of God removing trials out of our way to give us victory. God does promise victory, but He usually doesn't give us the time frame. This is when you really find out where your faith is. The victorious times are great, but what about the times when we feel like Daniel who was placed in the lion's den, or David, who was hunted by King Saul to be killed, or even Joseph, who was thrown in jail for doing the right thing? How about Moses who had to wander 40 years in the desert because of everyone else's fear and sin!

Life isn't about being fair; it's about being holy. It doesn't seem fair that all these seemingly bad things happened to God's people – even today. It doesn't seem fair that Jesus, who lived a perfect life, had to die such an extreme death. Some of the things you are going through may not seem fair. You cannot focus on what you think is fair or unfair; you have to focus on Jesus and trust Him in the middle of your trials.

Count on Him!!! If you follow by faith and believing, you are doing what God is calling you to do, He will provide victory in your life and in that situation. Here are some keys to help you through the challenge: seek God in prayer always, read the Bible daily, talk with Godly Christian friends because they are an incredible blessing from the Lord, set your hope on things above, and write down your thoughts and questions for God. Remember, there is no condemnation for those who are in Christ, so let His power lead you through.

Prayer:

"Lord Jesus, I believe in You. I trust in You, and I look forward to becoming more like You through the trials I face today and in the future. Just as the one man said in the Bible – I do have faith, but please increase my faith. Amen."

 **Application Questions:**

1. Have you thanked your close friends and/or family members recently for supporting you?

2. Do you realize the God of miracles you read about is the same God who helps you now?

3. Do you really trust God above your own efforts?

4. What do you need to surrender to God and trust Him for today?

5. How much do you love God?

6. Do you believe you are called according to God's purpose?

7. How well are you following that purpose today?

Action Plan:

One of the best things you can do when going through a challenge is to help someone else. Satan's trick is to get you focused on yourself to start a pity party. That is not God's will! It's exactly opposite of God's will. An example to illustrate this is in Exodus. When God's people had a pity party, they ended up wandering the desert for 40 years. God's will is for you to be thankful for what you do have. One of the best ways to do this is to help someone else. I encourage you to volunteer at your church, a food bank, a nursing home, or any place where there are people in great need. There is always something you can do – don't limit yourself. As you begin to focus on helping others, you will find your own worries shrink, and many times go away, as God does His thing in, to, and through you.

20 REAL CHRISTIANITY

Believing who Christ is doesn't make you a Christian but believing enough to surrender does.

Acts 11:26 "...So for a whole year Barnabas and Saul met with the church and taught great numbers of people. The disciples were called Christians first at Antioch."

Recent polls suggest that nearly 80% Americans consider themselves to be Christians. With just over 300,000,000 people now living in the United States, that would mean 240,000,000 of them are Christians. Let's think about this. If that many people were truly Christians, we wouldn't have nearly as much violence, murder, incest, drug abuse, alcoholism, family abuse, pornography, and other evils in our country.

In order to explain this point we first have to define what a Christian really is. In Acts 11, Disciples of Christ were first called Christians. Bible dictionaries simply define a Christian as "the name given to a follower of Christ" which would make sense since a disciple is "a person who follows the teaching and the teacher." The Hayford Bible Handbook makes a powerful statement that "In many modern societies, the original character of the name Christian has been emptied of its meaning as a biblical disciple of Christ."

Just because someone plays basketball, doesn't mean he or she is a basketball player (who depends on the sport for his or her livelihood). By the same token, just because someone goes to church or even reads the Bible, does not make him or her a Christian (someone who "follows the teaching and the teacher").

To really know if you are a Christian you need to look deep within to the core of your heart and spirit to see what is there. Better yet, ask God to show you very clearly. It doesn't matter who you say you are, what matters is who you really are and who you live for.

Do not fear walking with the God of the entire universe. If you already walk closely with Him, never give up that purpose as your reason for being and doing all that you do in life. If you aren't a true disciple, but claim to be Christian, you're deceiving yourself. Until you surrender everything to Christ, He is not Lord of your life. Only when you have emptied out all of yourself to Him can He fill you up and lead you into the incredible life and victory He has already laid out for you!

Prayer:

"Lord Jesus, please forgive me for the areas of my life that I have not turned over to You. Please forgive me if I have claimed to be a Christian in Your name but have not committed everything to You. I will follow You and Your teaching. Help me to take each step with You, in boldness and confidence, not fearing man but trusting in Your divine plan for my life. Amen."

 **Application Questions:**

1. What haven't you surrendered to God yet?

2. In what areas of your life are you living a lie by not turning them over to God?

3. Who will you talk with this week to confess your shortfalls and commit all to God?

4. What does it mean to you to be a true disciple of Jesus?

5. When is the last time you laid everything out bare before Christ?

6. How do you define "Christian"?

7. Are you the Christian that you defined above?

Action Plan:

Saying you're a Christian and being a Christian can be two different things. Ask yourself (and God), "Have I surrendered every area of my life over to Jesus Christ, and do I walk with Him daily?" If your answer is "no", then ask yourself why you have not made that decision? Now, if you are ready to make that full commitment, Christ is waiting with open arms. Confess your sins to Him and ask Him to take over every area and commit to spend daily time together. You will also need some support through a good Christian church, small group, or friend. If you are not ready to make that full commitment yet, Christ waits for you; so at least pray and ask Jesus what stands in your way. Ask others to pray for you as well (also see the "Do you know Jesus?" section above). If your answer is "yes", then you are a Christian who, is as it says above, "follows the teaching and the teacher." Continue to surrender and follow each day until the day you are with Him eternally in heaven.

21

CRASH!
When you are in life's tidal waves, don't forget about your life jacket.

Romans 8:39 "Nothing can separate you from the love of Christ."

Claudia and I had taken a trip to Mexico City for a family wedding, and afterward we stayed in Acapulco. Acapulco is a beautiful city on a bay on the Pacific coast, and the condo we stayed in was straight in from the mouth of the bay. The current funneling into the bay causes some wicked waves that can range between 8 –10 feet tall and crash right near shore in shallow water.

Claudia and I made the "brilliant" decision to rent wave runners. It was a lot of fun until we tried to come back to shore. The owner of the wave runner swam out to help us come in but unfortunately he was too short to reach the handle bars with both of us on the machine. Then I heard this fatal-sounding question – "Señor, can you swim?" I answered in my best American tough guy voice, "Swim. Of course I can swim". He asked me to jump off and swim to shore so he could take Claudia in. Being the hero that I am, I jumped off and started swimming. Then I realized that was not a good place to be! Rule #1 if a little Mexican guy ever asks if you can swim, say, "No, I can't, but my spouse can" (just kidding Claudia).

I was doing well swimming in and was thinking I would be fine getting back. Then a wave slammed me straight into the sand and spun me around as if I were in a washing machine. I didn't know where up, down, left or right were. Finally I popped out after what felt like 10 minutes. I thanked God that I had survived and was washing to shore. I was still a good 30 yards away when I saw a man signaling me to go back to the deep. Then horror came. I realized I was being sucked back into the ocean. I tried to grab onto sand with my fingernails. It didn't work! I looked behind me and saw the granddaddy of all waves forming. I still couldn't catch my breath, but I had no choice. "Crash" – right on top of me! This time I disappeared from everyone's sight for a while. I finally made it to shore, looking like the Castaway and feeling like a dead fish.

Once I caught my breath (an hour later), I confronted the little Mexican guy who pushed me off, I mean, asked me to swim. He apologized and said he knew I would be OK because I had my life jacket on. I thought about it and realized that's what saved me. It always caused me to rise back to the top of the water. Then I realized – Jesus is our life jacket of life. It does not matter what you go through, He is with you. He will never leave you nor forsake you and will always cause you to rise back to the top, even when you are thrown around by life like a limp rag doll. Whether it's your finances, your health, your job, your relationships, or anything else that's overwhelming, hold your "spiritual" breath, trust in the Lord, and He will bring you to shore!

Prayer:
"Lord Jesus, I trust You. Whatever I go through – I trust You! Whatever storms of life come my way, You are Lord of them, and I know You will not allow any waves to overwhelm me. Amen."

Application Questions:

1. Have you ever had waves in life cause you to feel overwhelmed and out of control?

2. What does it mean to you that nothing can separate you from the love of Christ?

3. Do you trust in Jesus or are you fighting life's waves on your own?

4. Who do you turn to when you can't tell up from down or left from right?

5. Do you feel Jesus' love, no matter what you are going through?

6. Are you in some of life's waves unnecessarily (because of how you are living)?

7. Is your first response to life's challenges to pray?

Action Plan:

Think about the last wicked wave you were hit by or about one you are struggling to escape out of now. Consider your "true" life jacket and how it did (or will) save you. When you are caught up in the waves of life, do what you can by not panicking and by trusting in the Lord. Think as you would if you were in a real wave. Think of ways to "hold your breath" through a situation and to start your "walk to shore". Finally, it's important to make sure your life vest is securely on. Rank these areas from 1–10 in your life: How often are you reading and using God's Word? How often are you listening for God's voice? Do you have a close Christian in your life who encourages you and can wave you to shore? For any area that is not at least an 8, make a plan to improve it.

22 HOW TRUE IT IS

It is important that you know, believe in, and live by the truth about you and about God.

Joshua 1:8 "Keep this Book of the Law always on your lips; meditate on it day and night, so that you may be careful to do everything written in it. Then you will be prosperous and successful."

There was a TV game show many years ago called "To Tell the Truth" in which four celebrities sat on a panel and listened to three people tell stories about their lives, their jobs and other personal areas. Two of the contestants made up lies, while one was sworn to tell the truth. The goal of the celebrities was to pick the person who was really telling the truth.

As Christians, doesn't it sometimes feel like our lives are that game show? We have three voices that go through our minds – God's, Satan's, and our own. God will always tell the truth, Satan will always lie, and our own voice many times deceives us. As believers in Christ it is important that we place our faith in what is true in every area of our lives. Christ tells us that He is the way, the truth, and the life and that no man comes to the Father but by Him.

So why is living by truth so important? You can find the answer in the beginning of time when God created Adam and Eve. The Garden of Eden was paradise and everything was good. God walked directly with Adam and Eve in the cool of day. However, something changed all this. Something really big happened. There was a lie told to Eve, who acted on it. Then the same lie was presented to Adam, who also acted on it, and from that day forward, paradise was no longer available to this couple or to any of us.

If you believe one lie and base your decisions on it, it can change the course of your life, your family's life, a nation or even a race of people forever. How many lies do we believe? The answer is probably countless. We believe wrong things about ourselves based on what other people tell us. We believe wrong things about others based on our own perceptions of them or what we hear about them. We believe wrong things about God based on our own life experience or even our relationship with our earthly father.

God directs us to live by faith while Satan's biggest trick is to use our faith to make us believe something completely false to limit our lives, cause fear, doubt God, and even miss His plan. Let God challenge and change the areas of your life you don't have peace in. Search for His truth through prayer, knowing God's Word, and affirming God's Word by the way you live.

Prayer:

"Lord God, show me Your way and Your truth. Help me throw all other things aside. I know that Satan comes to steal, kill, and destroy, but You come to bring life and bring it abundantly to me. Help me to walk in the freedom of Your truth day-by-day and moment-by-moment and to disregard everything that is false. Amen."

Application Questions:

1. Where do you turn for your source of truth for all things in life?

2. What truth did Jesus use when being tempted by Satan in the desert?

3. How well do you know God's Word and God's truth?

4. How well do you stand on, live by, and obey God's truth in your life?

5. Do you believe things about yourself that make you feel bad about who you are?

6. Do you believe anything about another person that could be untrue or is not Godly?

7. Do you believe anything about God, Christ, or His power that limits His plan for you?

Action Plan:

Think of all the different areas of your life (health, finances, relationships, self-image, etc.) by going through them one by one in your mind and asking God to reveal His truth to you. As you think and pray about each area, do you feel peace? If you are living by God's truth, it doesn't mean every area is exactly where you want it to be, but it does mean you are living it to the best of your ability by following God's Word by faith. If there is any area(s) about which you do not feel peace – why is that? What is it that you do not believe in, not trusting God for, or not applying His Word to? Take those areas and look on-line, in your Bible, or at a Bible promise book to find scriptures to see what God's truth says about it. Finally, talk with a Christian friend (preferably an accountability partner) about a plan on how to begin to live by faith in that area of your life and ask him or her to pray for you and hold you accountable.

23 HOW TO REALLY COMMUNICATE WITH GOD

If you want to have a better relationship with God it must be intentional.

Matthew 6:9–13 "This, then, is how you should pray: 'Our Father in heaven, hallowed be your name, your kingdom come, your will be done, on earth as it is in heaven. Give us today our daily bread. And forgive us our debts, as we also have forgiven our debtors. And lead us not into temptation, but deliver us from the evil one.'"

Communication in life is more important than we think. Without communication we would have no relationships! I know there are days when this sounds like a good thing. However, a good reminder of how miserable it would be with no one else in your life is to watch (or re-watch) the movie Castaway with Tom Hanks.

God designed us to have relationships and to communicate with Him and each other. True communication does mean audible words. A great friend of mine named Drake has a daughter named Danel who is deaf and they communicate better in their relationship than most hearing people do in theirs. Why is this? It's because they know each other's hearts. They feel what each other feels, and they can sense the needs and desires of each other because they are so close. They know each other's likes and dislikes. They put each other first and take time to understand the other's points of view, which can be done without words. They are not critical but love and support each other. They find many ways to communicate their love and support in a deeper way than words. Amazingly, Drake's whole family communicates on a deeper level than words.

To communicate well with God you need to know Him on a deep level. This isn't just by listening to sermons on Sundays. When you really put Him first by taking time to know Him through His Word, prayer, and His Holy Spirit, you will know and have the Father's heart. If you want a deep relationship with God, it must be intentional! Only by opening up your heart to Jesus, by laying out your hopes, hurts, feelings, and deep things in you, can you build a much closer relationship with Him. He is committed to an intimate relationship with you.

The best way to know and "walk with God" (as Enoch did) is to read His letter to us, the Bible, and pray by being real with Him. Pour your heart out to God; don't just be superficial, because He wants to love you on a deep level. Take time to be quiet and listen so you learn to hear Him and know Him deeply. His still small voice will bring peace and direction to your life. True relationships require time together, so be sure to open up to Him daily. These are the elements of any truly deep and meaningful relationship with God or anyone else in your life.

Prayer:

"Lord Jesus, I love You. I don't just want things from You; I want to know You deeply. I want to pray as David prayed, not just words but from the heart. I believe in You and know that You are with me always. I want to walk with You day-by-day and moment-by-moment. Speak to me Lord; show me more of You. My heart is open, and I commit to know more. Amen."

 **Application Questions:**

1. How well do you know God's heart?

2. How well do you open up your heart to God?

3. How has God spoken to you in the past?

4. When is the last time you heard God speak?

5. What commitment have you made to God in building your relationship?

6. Do you build Godly, loving relationships with anyone else?

7. Will you completely open up your heart to God and listen for what He has to say to you?

Action Plan:

Think about your closest relationship here on earth. What makes it so close? Think about the amount of time you spend with this person, how frequently you communicate, how open you are with him or her, and how well you know each other's likes and dislikes. Also consider what situations and experiences have helped you get so close. Make a list of the top five things that have helped you grow close (it may have been dedicating time to talk, praying for each other, helping each other through life struggles, struggles against each other, or whatever else comes to mind). Is your relationship with Jesus closer than that human relationship? Take the five things that helped you build that human relationship and prioritize them based on the greatest impact to help you grow close. For the next five weeks make a plan on how to use each of these to build your relationship with Jesus.

THROUGH CHRIST

If you can do all things through Christ, make sure you are led by Christ to do them.

Philippians 4:13 "I can do all this through Him who gives me strength."

Have you noticed there are "popular" scriptures that hit home for lots of Christians at different points in time? For example, several years ago Jeremiah 29:11 was quoted everywhere and helped encourage believers to trust in and follow God's plan for their lives.

More recently Philippians 4:13 has become popular among Christians. You may know people who claim this verse but have no positive results in their lives. I know some Christians who for years have firmly believed in a huge vision from God yet have not been paying their bills, have not taken care of responsibilities, and are, therefore, not bearing fruit. Don't get me wrong, there are times that all of us go through when we believe the blessing of God is coming, but we can see that it is being delayed. However, many "believers" are standing on their own thoughts, ambitions, and desires, claiming God will do miracles to achieve what they want.

The verse above (Phil 4:13) needs to be used by referencing the verse before it (Phil 4:12) where Paul talks about being content in every situation. Paul had already experienced many victories, including seeing and hearing the risen Christ and leading multitudes to salvation. He also had intense difficulties like beatings, stonings, a shipwreck, and jail, just to name a few. All this was for the sake of Christ. Paul then realized he really could do all things through Christ who was his strength.

The problem that can arise with quoting Philippians 4:13 is we can falsely believe we can do whatever we want through Christ who strengthens us. If you look closer at Paul's life you will see that everything he went through was orchestrated by the Holy Spirit. Many times God led him to or away from situations, cities, and people.

You truly can do all things through Christ who strengthens you when you make sure it is God who is calling you to do it. This scripture does not apply if your direction is coming from your own ideas, others opinions, or temptations from the evil one. You can know you are being led by Christ by spending time in prayer, asking God for confirmation, and making sure it agrees with God's Word. When you are walking with Christ step by step, you can rest assured that God's good and perfect will will come to pass in your life. You can then stand firmly on faith that you can and will do all things through Christ who strengthens you.

Prayer:
"Lord God almighty, You are the maker of heaven and earth. You have the world at Your fingertips and my life in the palm of Your hands. Help me believe more than ever in Your love for me, Your power in my life, and Your good and perfect will to be completed through me. Increase my faith in You by showing me Your will, and I will follow because I know and believe that I can do all things through You who strengthens me. Amen."

Application Questions:

1. Where and how do you get your strength to live each day?

2. How often per day do you turn to Jesus as your source for strength?

3. Do you believe that you can do all things through Christ?

4. When you face a Goliath in life, how much do you rely on Christ for victory?

5. What will you do today as a step of faith?

6. What do you believe God will do through Christ in the impossible situations in your life?

7. Are you getting all your direction from Christ so you can stand firm on Phil 4:13?

Action Plan:

Think of a current situation (possibly a significant one), or one that will be coming, that requires a decision to be made. Depending on the time you have before you must make this decision, try these steps (in order) to see how God leads you. First, spend 15 minutes today in prayer specifically for this topic. Write down your question on paper then wait to see what God shows you about it. Then write that down also. Next write down any scriptures that apply to this situation on the same paper. Do the scriptures agree or disagree with what you feel God was showing you? Next recruit a Christian friend to pray for you (you may or may not give details to them, but God knows the situation). If the decision is big and you have a couple days, then don't jump to the decision, but ask God for a confirmation. Also, consider fasting (not eating) for a meal or a day in order to focus on God by sacrificing your personal wants and needs to hear God's voice.

25 PERFECT STORMS

The storms of life will come but how you choose to face them will determine your outcome.

Matthew 11:28-30 "Come to me, all you who are weary and burdened, and I will give you rest. Take my yoke upon you and learn from me, for I am gentle and humble in heart, and you will find rest for your souls. For my yoke is easy and my burden is light."

In the true life movie The Perfect Storm a group of fishermen are out in their boat on a day when three major storms collide in the Atlantic Ocean. The day the storm hit, these fishermen were out at sea on a beautifully sunny day with calm water. They heard the report of major storms coming, but instead of turning to land and safety, they chose to risk their very survival in search of prosperity – a huge catch of fish. This decision ended up costing them their lives.

There are some big lessons we can learn from this story. The first lesson is that we will face storms, even at times when we are cruising along on a nice, sunny day. Storms and challenges in life are unpredictable and inevitable – Jesus said so.

The second lesson is that we must turn to Christ when storms approach. None of these men appeared to be Christians and did not ask God for direction. They made decisions based on their own wisdom and experience and perished because of it. Here is the key – don't pick to be in storms you should not be in. These men made the wrong choice. You have choices to make in life. Spend time to hear God's voice so the storms of life you go through are used by Him to build you up, not picked by you to lead to destruction.

The final lesson from this story is we are not to fear anything in life when following Jesus. If God has allowed you to be in a storm and you're following in faith, do not fret, you will see great victory! If you put yourself in a storm by not following God's path, there is also good news. He will lead you to victory if you surrender all to follow Him. The recovery may be challenging, and may take time to "undo" your mistake, relearn, and build your trust in God! The sooner you surrender all, the sooner you will have peace to know Jesus will lead you to His victory.

In the military they teach sailors who are prone to seasickness to take their eyes off the waves and focus on a fixed point on the horizon. By focusing on something solid and immovable the waves become manageable. What do you focus on in the midst of life's storms? If it is something movable, you'll get sick and be overcome. If you focus on Christ, (The fixed light on the horizon) you will not only weather the storm, but also come out closer to Him and stronger in the end.

Prayer:

"Lord God, I love You. Help me to keep my focus on You. As David was a man after Your own heart, help me to be a person after Your heart. Let all things in my life be led by You. When I face the trials and storms, help me to focus on and follow You in faith. Help me to grow closer to You so my life will reflect You to this world. In Jesus Christ's name I pray, Amen."

Application Questions:

1. What do you focus on when you face storms?

2. Is the storm you're currently facing (or recently faced) occurring because of bad choices?

3. Is the storm you're currently facing (or recently faced) occurring because God simply allowed it?

4. Have you surrendered everything to God?

5. In your current storms, are you looking for God and listening to His voice?

6. Do you have peace in the middle of your storm?

7. Who is a fellow Christian "sailor" who can help support you through the storm?

Action Plan:

This is a three-part action plan. The first part is to check your attitude. What is one word you would use to describe how you face storms in life when they come? Keep in mind that we are to have the attitude of Christ. If you don't have the right attitude, what is one thing you can do to change it? Second, do you know if your storms are from God's plan or from wrong choices? Have faith; even if the storm you are in is from bad, ungodly choices, He will help you if you follow Him. Learn from any storms that were from bad decisions, and ask Christ to help you avoid them in the future. Finally, rank the level of your faith 1–10 during the storms with 10 being high. What do you need to do to surrender to Christ and believe? Remember, you only need to have the faith of a child that God is with you (because He is). Also, the Bible tells us that Jesus honors your request when you ask Him to increase your faith.

26 WHAT ARE YOU WAITING FOR?

We were waiting for you.
Why didn't you come?

Romans 14:23 "Anything not done in faith is sin."

How quickly do you follow Jesus when He asks you to do something? I am sure we can all think of times in our lives when God has asked us to do something and we dragged our feet because of fear or doubt. We may have later regretted those decisions not to act because we eventually realized that we could have missed the chance to make a change in our life, a chance to walk in faith, or even more importantly – missed the chance to minister to someone in need.

I will never forget a testimony given by a missionary who missed his timing. He was living in Texas at the time when God told him to drive to Galeana, Mexico with his family in the bus that they lived and traveled in. God spoke to his heart saying that he was to drive to the outskirts of this little Mexican town, then God would send someone to him to show him where he and his family were to stay and minister. He was excited and nervous about this call from God and told some of his Christian friends. They were very concerned for his travel, especially because of the condition of the two front tires of his bus.

His friends warned that he should not travel with bad tires, so he waited. After two weeks one of his friends provided one of the tires for the bus, and a couple of weeks later the other tire was provided. At that point one month had gone by, and the missionary was still in Texas. Then he happened to run into a woman from Mexico, specifically Galeana. Without telling her his whole story, her appearance became somber as she spoke with him. Finally she looked him straight in the eyes with a serious expression and said "We were waiting for you. Why didn't you come?"

Wow, doesn't that hit home? God told him to go. His friends and his fear told him to wait. That whole time God had been speaking to those in Galeana, telling them that someone would soon be arriving to minister to them. The biggest lesson for us to learn from this is to listen for God's voice and to do whatever He calls us to do. Just as a note, this doesn't mean we jump into whatever thought pops into our minds without letting God confirm it is His leading. But when you feel that nudge in your spirit and the confidence that Jesus is leading you, listen to His direction and follow. Others may be depending on it.

Prayer:

"Lord Jesus, You are the God of all, and You see all of history and all the future at one time. You know the hairs of my head, the plans You have for me, and the number of my days on this earth. Show me more of You and Your plan for my life. Lead me along Your path. Give me the courage and faith to follow you everywhere You call me to be. Amen."

 **Application Questions:**

1. What is one thing God has called or is calling you to do?

2. Are you being faithful in following God's call in every area of your life right now?

3. How quickly do you follow Jesus when He asks you to do something?

4. Who has the most influence in your life (God, yourself, friends, family)?

5. What has held you back in the past from following Him?

6. Could you handle hearing the words – "Why didn't you do what God called you to do?"

7. Who do you know that lives by faith in every area of his or her life?

 **Action Plan:**

Think of something God is currently calling you to do or has recently put on your heart to do. This could be to take a step of faith in your personal life, business life, in reconciling with someone, or in giving up something in your life. Maybe it's even a step to get help in overcoming a sin area of your life. Whatever it is, how long has God been calling you to take action? What is holding you back? The biggest question you need to ask yourself is if you are really willing to follow Jesus in all things and at all times. If you're willing to follow Him then ask Him what you need to remove or put in place to follow. If you are in the middle of a situation that you are avoiding and you really want to walk with Jesus, commit to Jesus today exactly when you will take the steps. The sooner the better. He will bless you for it! If you are not in a situation like this right now, ask God to lead you by faith and the next prompting you get from Him, do it! It will change your life and your walk with him.

27 JOYFUL TRIALS

When you face trials, do you focus on the trial or on the Father who will bring you through it?

James 1:2 "Consider it pure joy, my brothers, whenever you face trials of many kinds, because you know that the testing of your faith develops perseverance. Perseverance must finish its work so that you may be mature and complete, not lacking anything."

Just after I got out of college and moved to Florida, I began attending a new church and soon found powerful examples of James 1:2 that changed my life. I started attending a men's Bible Study, and I met two men who were both in their 70's. The first was a retired pastor who had health and financial struggles, but you would never know it by his attitude. He was one of the most joyful and happy men I have ever met because he trusted God implicitly in every situation. Another man I met, who was the same age, really had no current struggles but was always negative and pessimistic. He actually was miserable compared to the man with all the problems.

I couldn't understand why the vast difference in these two men who both grew up in the same era and same country. Then God showed me that all through their lives these men faced trials, and they chose their attitudes through each situation. The older they got, the stronger their attitude became (positive or negative). It brought one man to a very close walk with God that was filled with joy. It brought the other man to a miserable state because he focused on worry and doubt.

When you are in the middle of a tough trial, you will find that most every part of that trial is out of your control. God does not ask you to control the trial or the circumstance. He does, however, ask you to control what you can – your attitude! Your attitude is a choice in every situation you face in life. By choosing a Godly attitude and trusting in your Lord Jesus to see you through it, you are walking in faith. To worry, doubt, complain, and try to make your own way is sin.

So how can we live like the first elderly man to face trials in life with joy? At first it can be a challenge to not focus on the problem, but the Father. Remember, this passage does not say to consider the trial itself a joy. But when you are faced with a trial, God will do a work in you and change you through the trial. He counts you worthy to face that challenge in your life because your faith in Him is strong enough. You may not think your faith is strong, but God promises He will not allow you to be tested beyond what you can bear. Face your trial with joy in the Lord, and the result will be spiritual maturity and a closer walk with God than you have ever had.

Prayer:

"Lord Jesus, I LOVE YOU. I pray for Your divine guidance to light my path and for Your Holy Spirit to strengthen me as I walk with You. I know that I will have trials and challenges, but I pray for increased faith so I may face them in joy with full faith and assurance that You will see me through and that Your will will be accomplished by making me mature and complete."

 **Application Questions:**

1. What are some of the trials you are facing right now in your life?

2. What is your attitude toward these trials?

3. How can you keep a positive attitude and trust in God today?

4. What do you need to focus on through your trials to grow closer to Christ?

5. What has God been showing you through these situations?

6. Who in your life is a Godly example of going through trials by faith?

7. Who can you ask to pray for you and support you through your trials?

Action Plan:

Let's first take an assessment! Think of the last challenging situation you went through or the one you're currently in. What was your very first response to the situation? If it was negative, complaining, or worrying, you may be in that situation for a long time. The Israelites complained, and they wandered the desert forty years. If your response was going to your knees and trusting in God by rejoicing that He is in control – perfect! Now think of how you handled the challenge after your initial reaction. Even if you had a good attitude to start but then soon became bitter, that is not Godly. Here is a simple, two-step process to handle life's challenges. During your daily time with God write down what's on your mind. Next, pray to release that challenge to God and continue to pray until you have peace in your spirit. When you give your problem to Him each day, leave it with Him and rejoice in the day you have because it is the Lord's day of victory for you!

28 NEVER GIVE UP!

Unless God says it's over, it's never over – do not give up your faith!

Revelation 21:7 "He that overcomes shall inherit these things; and I will be his God, and he shall be my son."

I remember the day I got a call from the husband of a very good friend of mine. The voicemail I received scared me because I knew something had to be wrong. My family was friends for many years with his wife's family; however, he and I were only casual friends, and we never called each other or talked on the phone. Even more heart wrenching was that the call came from across the country, and the voicemail sounded something like "Hi Brian, this is Jen's husband. Hopefully you remember me. Please give me a call; I have something I need to tell you."

I immediately called Rich back, and he picked up the phone. I asked if everything was OK. He said, "Yes, I just wanted to call and let you know that I accepted Jesus into my heart today." I immediately got chills. He thanked me for praying for him all these years. This was a man who was big and strong and always had a hard shell. Now I could hear the love of God in his voice. He said Christ was pulling on his heart for a long time, but he kept fighting it – until today. He went to church with his wife and kids to accept Christ because the people there had been praying for him for years. He thanked them for not giving up in praying for his salvation.

When Rich and Jen met, neither of them was living for Christ. Several years after they got married, Jen came back to Christ, but Rich was never a believer. There were many times over the years when Jen would call me crying and tell me how she had been pleading with God for her husband to open his heart to Christ. At times it seemed impossible that he would ever change. However, she clung to a promise God gave her that Rich would one day surrender. It is hard to comprehend the powerful impact this child of God had on her husband because she fought for him spiritually against the fears, worries, and doubts of her emotions. She got on her knees daily for nearly 20 years, holding onto God's promise and now saw her husband reborn!

What are you praying for? What is God having you trust in Him for that seems like hoping against hope? Don't give up! If God promised it, although it may take all that is within you to hold on, BELIEVE! Trust in the God who brought Israel out of slavery, had a 100 year old woman give birth, and came to earth to die for you so you would be able to have victory in every area of life. Stay on your knees until you see God's promise come to pass in your life, and ask another Child of God you know to believe with you!

Prayer:

"Lord Jesus, help me trust in You for all things regardless of how they look. I believe you will do what you promise. Amen."

 **Application Questions:**

1. What do you believe is too big for your God?

2. Do you have a promise from God to hold on to?

3. What scripture(s) backs up God's promise to you?

4. Who is standing with you in prayer?

5. Will you stand today on God's promises?

6. How willing are you to persevere and trust only in God and His will?

7. What is important enough to you to get on your knees and pray about daily for 20 years?

 Action Plan:

I highly recommend that you write the answers down to the following so you can refer to it in times of worry or doubt. Think of a hope or dream God has given you. Let's first make sure the dream is from God and not from you or the pizza you ate the night before. Think about when God gave you the hope or dream, where you were, and what you were doing. How and when has God reaffirmed this for you? Even more importantly is to find a scripture(s) that is God's promise for you about this hope you have. You can do this by using a Bible promise book or the index of your Bible. If you are now clear about your hope or dream, and have a promise from God to back it up, you should be praying about this every day! This may not mean God will call you to take steps on it right now, but it does mean you are trusting in Him for His purpose and standing strong on Him, not your own vision or belief. Finally, also write down the names of all the saints around you that you have recruited to also pray for this in your life.

29 WHY ME, LORD?

To have fullness of life, start asking 'Why Me, Lord?' for a better reason

Philippians 2:5 "Your attitude should be the same as that of Christ Jesus."

I sent out a questionnaire to hundreds of people a while back asking what topic they would most like help on in life. One of the responses I got back was "Why me, Lord?" I thought it was a little funny, knowing the person who wrote it, yet I believe it is a very important question to discuss.

Don't we all find ourselves from time to time asking, "Why me, Lord"? If you answered "no", then you obviously also struggle with the sin of lying. On a serious note, we don't see the big picture in life, and when we are caught in the middle of what we were hoping for and what we see happening, we can't help but question God. It is not wrong to question God, but it is wrong to doubt Him (see the book of Job).

When do you find yourself asking "Why me, Lord?" Most of us seem to ask this when life is falling apart. We question God when sickness or disease comes, when we lose a job, or when finances are falling apart. It could be because a lifelong dream is failing and nothing seems to be happening. I'm sure you can come up with your list of things that cause you to ask the question, and it's a valid question!

Let me offer a complete change of perspective. When you are tempted to ask God the "why" question, first ask Him why He loves you so much, even with all of your faults and doubts. You should also ask why He went to the cross for you before you were even born and why He has blessed you so much to live in the 20th century compared to other barbaric times. Even more importantly (for most reading this) we should ask why God has allowed us to live where we are free to worship Christ publicly. A humbling question I find myself asking is "Why does Christ always stand by my side even when I forget to include Him in so many things?" God's grace is amazing!

We can ask God why things are so tough and why he allows such struggles, but don't forget to also ask why He has blessed you in so many other ways even in the midst of huge trials. You may find you have been asking "why" for the wrong reason, and I challenge you to change your question from "why" to "'how' can I serve you Lord, even in the midst of the trial?"

Prayer:

"Lord, help me to change my thinking. I know I can be so selfish and focused on me. Lord Jesus, help me to focus on You. I don't know why You love me so much, I don't know why You have blessed me so much, and I don't know why You entrust me to share Your good news, but I thank You. Please show me how I can live for You and serve You today by showing my love for You to others. In the name of Jesus Christ I pray. Amen."

 **Application Questions:**

1. How often do you ask, "Why me, Lord?"

2. Do you usually ask "why" because of desperation or thankfulness?

3. How can you change your question from self-serving to God serving?

4. Do you actually doubt God is with you and has a perfect plan?

5. Who is a grateful person in your life who can help encourage you?

6. If God never answers your "Why me?" question, can you move forward and trust him?

7. How can you serve the Lord, even in the midst of the trial?

 **Action Plan:**

There are many things in life we will not know the answers to until we go to be with Jesus. When you realize this, how does it make you feel, and are you willing to trust in God, for now, even if you don't have all the answers? Don't fall into the misbelief that you will never get an answer, just consider it as delayed. You still may get the answer in a few weeks, months or years because sometimes God answers our "why" questions while we are still on earth. Now you may be at a crossroad. Consider this, until God answers your "why" question, are you willing to turn it into a "how" question by asking God "how" you can serve him now and do this with all of your heart? You will be surprised that by asking "how," then doing what God shows you, your "why" question becomes less of a stumbling block. You may even find by doing this your "how" question later answer your "why" question.

30 A SPECIAL GUEST

How well do you maintain your temple for the Holy Spirit who lives in you?

1 Corinthians 3:16–17 "Don't you know that you yourselves are God's temple and that God's Spirit dwells in your midst? If anyone destroys God's temple, God will destroy that person; for God's temple is sacred, and you together are that temple."

If you had a special guest come stay in your home, my guess is you would take pride in your place and keep it clean, well maintained, and looking beautiful. If anything needed repaired, you would be sure to put it in working order for his or her stay.

Now let's imagine this guest is a person you greatly admire. He or she has impacted your life and the lives of many others. It could be Billy Graham, Mother Theresa, Tony Dungy, or any other Godly person you greatly respect. How would you prepare your house for that person's stay and how would you treat them while they are staying with you? Most of us would do everything possible within our means to prepare for their coming and make their stay as welcoming as possible.

Before Christ came as a baby, there was a temple built for God that was made with the finest materials on earth and guarded with the strictest care. Around the clock this temple was highly esteemed and used to reconcile people unto God. If you have asked Jesus to come into your life as Lord and Savior, you are now that temple and your physical body is where the Holy Spirit now dwells. Think about that!

The God of the universe, who made you and everything you now see, resides in your physical body. He doesn't just visit you from time to time, he dwells inside you continually. The Spirit is your teacher and friend. He talks to you during His stay to direct your thoughts, words and actions according to God's will.

When you don't live according to God's will, you hurt (grieve) your guest – the Holy Spirit. It's your responsibility to only allow healthy and righteous things in your "temple". To take care of your temple is to take care of your physical body with overall healthy eating, physical activity and sleep. When you abuse your body, ask yourself, "How functional is this body to carry out God's plan?" It also means to guard what comes into your heart and mind! When you entertain, don't allow unrighteousness (things God doesn't approve of) in your mind that is degrading to your houseguest. Be proactive to take care of your temple the way you would your house with a special guest. The Holy Spirit will help you.

Prayer:

"Lord Jesus, thank You for who You made me to be. Your choice for me is perfect! I have made choices that haven't been glorifying to You. Help me to clean my temple out and get rid of anything offensive to you. Help me to make the most of this temple You gave me. Amen."

Application Questions:

1. Do you realize the importance of your physical body in relation to God's calling?

2. How well would you say you maintain the temple that God gave you?

3. What are you doing with your temple that would make the Holy Spirit uncomfortable?

4. What are you not doing with your temple that you should be?

5. What are you allowing into your mind that would make the Holy Spirit uncomfortable?

6. What are you not putting into your mind that you should be?

7. What will you begin changing now to take better care of your temple for the Holy Spirit?

Action Plan:

In order to make your body and mind a place where the Holy Spirit feels at home and wants first write down all the "rooms" of your life, such as: health, thinking, habits, finances, career, relationships, physical body, hobbies, attitude, and spiritual walk. Next, write down the things that are honoring to God in those "rooms." Then write down the things that are not pleasing to Him (including what you are neglecting) such as sin you are intentionally allowing and any areas that aren't holy. Are there any "secret rooms" you are avoiding? Pray and ask God what area to work on first, and then make a plan to improve. Remember, if this were your actual house, you might need a specialist to come in and repaint, make repairs, etc. This also applies spiritually as you may need to work with a Christian counselor, coach, financial planner, or an expert to help get your spiritual house in order. Amazingly, your guest will help you do it!

31

LISTEN

A true relationship with God involves not just asking, but also involves listening.

Psalm 65:2-4 "You who answer prayer, to you all people will come. When we were overwhelmed by sins, you forgave our transgressions. Blessed are those you choose and bring near to live in your courts! We are filled with the good things of your house, of your holy temple."

When I am listening for God I usually have to get very quiet (in my body, mind, and heart) before I can hear Him. One time I was listening and searching for weeks to know God's plan, and it seemed like eternity. Finally, one morning I felt God was going to speak, so I got ready to write. As God put the words in my heart, I wrote what He showed me – then felt complete peace about my next steps.

Below is an excerpt of what God revealed to me. He was very clear, and it spoke to my spirit and hopefully it will speak to yours also:

"This is a critical point in your life. The decisions you make now will impact the rest of your future. I will lead and guide you, but you must seek me. Listen to me as I instruct you. Anything that interferes with our relationship is not good, but everything that strengthens it is. Know how people, situations, and things impact you and your closeness to Me.

"This is the time for decisions, important decisions. You cannot walk by fear; you must walk by faith – faith in me and my perfect plan for your life. Your decisions are critical. Glorify me. Keep my children first in all the decisions you make, and love them as you love me. Do not look back, only look forward.

"You will grow as you focus on me! Work together in unity; listen to my voice as I lead you to lead others… unto me. Feed my sheep. What does it profit a man if he gains the whole world yet loses his soul? Everything you own is mine. Do not be afraid of losing anything; it was never yours in the first place. Trust in me and all the dreams, goals, and visions that I have put in your heart will come true."

There are many wise people in this world that you can listen to, but when you follow Jesus Christ with all your heart the only words that really matter are the ones that come from Him. If you haven't gotten your answers yet, keep seeking Him because He promises that you will find Him. Also, keep a pen and paper nearby so that as He reveals things to you, you will not forget and move on, but will be able to absorb and apply what He shows you.

Prayer:
"Speak to me Lord, for your child is here – listening and waiting for You. Amen."

 **Application Questions:**

1. What are you seeking God for in your life?

2. How long have you been listening for an answer?

3. How does God speak to you?

4. How much time do you spend quietly listening for God's still, small voice each day?

5. What is one time when you really heard (sensed) God clearly?

6. What different ways in the past has God shown you His plan and will?

7. Who can you ask to stand with you in prayer as you seek God?

Action Plan:

It is important not only to hear from God (through the Bible, His still small voice, other people, and various other ways), but also to remember what he showed you. Capturing His direction will not only help you grow and overcome now, but reviewing it in the future encourages your faith. The action step this week is to keep a small notebook, piece of paper, or smart phone with you, and every time God reveals something, answers a prayer, or is evident in a situation, write it down. After one week go back to review what you have written then see how this changes your perspective and faith for moving forward.

32 I LOVE YOU!

There are no words, no quotes and no lessons more powerful than 'I love you!'

Matthew 22:36–40 "'Teacher, which is the greatest commandment in the Law?' Jesus replied: 'Love the Lord your God with all your heart and with all your soul and with all your mind.' This is the first and greatest commandment. And the second is like it: 'Love your neighbor as yourself.' All the Law and the Prophets hang on these two commandments."

There are many great inspirational people we can learn from today. We can learn from others' examples in almost every area of life. There are movies and biographies about those who inspire and teach us about our "heroes" and what they accomplished. We always seem to be drawn to people who have done great things in hopes that we can one day do the same.

We also draw words of inspiration from great quotes that motivate us. Many of these men and women that we quote today lived many years ago. I am sure you recognize quotes like: "I have a dream," or "Ask not what your country can do for you but what you can do for your country." How about "Never, never, never, never give up," or "Mr. Gorbachev, tear down this wall," or "Mama always told me, life is like a box of chocolates" (How did that get in there?).

The bottom line is that we can learn quotes, skills, and strategies from others who have accomplished a lot in life. The Bible even tells us to do that. However, none of them compare to the greatest words ever spoken – "I love you!" Think about this. If you learned every great quote and tactic in history but never felt deeply loved, none of it would matter? God the Father, Son and Holy Spirit says to you right now where you are – "I love you!!!" It doesn't matter what you have (or have not) accomplished or what others opinions are of you. The God of all Creation loves you because you are you. He made you.

This truth is almost too big to comprehend especially knowing our many failures in life. Yet God keeps saying to each of us, "I Love You." All we can do is receive and accept Jesus' love – we cannot and have not earned it. When it permeates who we are, it will then flow out of us and to other people. It is God's greatest desire for us to "love the Lord your God with all your heart, soul, mind and strength" then to "love your neighbor as yourself."

You will achieve great things in life by following Christ and those He uses to teach you, but always remember that of all the seemingly great things in this world, only three remain to the very end: "faith, hope, and love." They will know you are a Christian by your love, so go out and give it away by praying for others, witnessing to others, and helping others!

Prayer:
"Lord Jesus, You not only say you love me but You also died for me because You love me. I don't understand the depth of Your love so help me to accept it, live according to it, and spread it to all others. I love you Lord. Please increase my love for You and others today! Amen."

 **Application Questions:**

1. Do you feel truly and deeply loved by God?

2. How much time are you spending with God and in His Word each day?

3. How well is God's love flowing through you to others?

4. Would people around you automatically know you are a Christian by your love?

5. What are the ways you give God's love to others?

6. How do you define love?

7. Does the way you define love agree with how God defines love?

 **Action Plan:**

Keep track of, for at least one day, the number of times you do something in life (whether large or small) out of love for God or someone else. The next day keep track of how many decisions you have made through the day out of selfishness, fear, or anything else besides love. How do the totals compare? Think of what you can do to remind yourself to make most (if not all) of your decisions based on love for God and for others vs. for your own selfish desires. When and how will you start doing this? Who in your life can help hold you accountable to this?

33

GROWING UP

Spiritual maturity is a choice;
God gives the opportunities
but you make the choice.

2 Peter 1:5–11 "For this very reason, make every effort to add to your faith goodness; and to goodness, knowledge; and to knowledge, self-control; and to self-control, perseverance; and to perseverance, godliness; and to godliness, mutual affection; and to mutual affection, love. For if you possess these qualities in increasing measure, they will keep you from being ineffective and unproductive in your knowledge of our Lord Jesus Christ. But whoever does not have them is nearsighted and blind, forgetting that they have been cleansed from their past sins. Therefore, my brothers and sisters, make every effort to confirm your calling and election. For if you do these things, you will never stumble, and you will receive a rich welcome into the eternal kingdom of our Lord and Savior Jesus Christ."

It's amazing as an adult to think back about our growing up years and the many things we went through to "mature" physically. We really went through a lot to grow up. You probably remember some great times as well as some major challenges (such as puberty, physical growing pains, etc.) that took everything within you to get through them. Physical maturity automatically happens whether you want it to or not.

We are also "supposed to" mature spiritually once we accept Christ as our Savior. However, unlike physical maturity, you can stop your progress of spiritual maturity. Imagine if a child's growth was optional. You could have a baby that you carry around in your arms for 20 years because it refuses to grow up. The maturity process of a Christian is spelled out in 2 Peter 1:5-11 and is "optional" based on your own choices.

In the stages of spiritual growth, ranging from faith and goodness to godliness and love, there are some tough stages where most people get stuck, and therefore they remain spiritual babies. Those sticking points are "self-control" and "perseverance". Let's face it, it's pretty easy to say we have faith and even say we try to be good Christians. However, the bridge between the simple basics and really becoming godly is a challenging walk through temptation and trials.

When you were a child growing and maturing through tough and painful experiences regarding relationships, emotions, body, etc. you may have chosen not to go through these things if given the choice back then. God knew that, so he made it mandatory and you grew because of it. Spiritual maturity is a choice and most Christians pick pleasure and avoid pain. The problem then becomes stagnation. Only through overcoming temptations and persevering through trials will you experience true spiritual growth. The choice is yours to either stay a "baby" or walk God's course and follow His plan to mature in Christ.

Prayer:

"Lord, help me to grow up in You. I want to be all that You have called me to be. Help me to have self-control and to persevere to become more like You every day. Amen."

Application Questions:

1. How do you face trials and temptations?

2. How important is it for you to grow up spiritually?

3. In what areas have you fallen instead of having self-control?

4. Do you desire to mature by controlling yourself when temptations come?

5. When and in what areas do you find you give up instead of persevere?

6. Do you want to become godly so much you're willing to persevere through pain?

7. Who is the spiritually mature person in your life who can keep you on track?

Action Plan:

Review the scripture above in 2 Peter and note which step(s) along this spiritual growth cycle trips you up most of the time. Why is this area so difficult for you to grow in? If you are ready to mature and grow in Christ, it is time to confront this stumbling block. First, recognize it is your choice – the ball is in your court and no one can make the choice for you to grow and mature. You must ask yourself if you are determined to mature in your walk with Jesus. If you are ready to mature, then think about 1-3 things you can do differently in your life to overcome and succeed in this area. To get good ideas you might ask Christian friends what they do to overcome, read books by Spiritual leaders you respect about how they live their lives, and read the Bible and ask God for wisdom. It is important to have a prayer partner (since this a spiritual battle that Satan doesn't want you to win) and an accountability partner or coach to support you.

34

HOW TO FIX A COUNTRY!

Follow God and follow leaders who follow God!

2 Chronicles 7:13 "If my people, who are called by my name, will humble themselves and pray and seek my face and turn from their wicked ways, then will I hear from heaven and will forgive their sin and will heal their land. Now my eyes will be open and my ears attentive to the prayers offered in this place."

What an amazing time we now live in. We are watching history as America, the world power, struggles for each breath of air. In everything from finance to politics there are huge challenges and battles.

If you were the President, how would you handle America's complex problems? You'd have to deal with a collapsing economy, an exhaustive war, worldwide struggles, moral battles, and a broken healthcare system. All of your decisions would impact hundreds of millions of people in this country and billions worldwide. When you put yourself in the place of this leader, there's no easy choice. However, God still has and is the answer.

Here is the answer – follow 2 Chronicles 7:13–15. This is what the Bible says our country and any country have to do to experience complete victory in all areas. Simply put, there are absolute answers to all the problems we currently face – some miraculous (direct from God) and others led through the decisions of leaders as they hear from God.

If you look back at the history of Israel, when there were good leaders that followed God the nation was blessed. Even against impossible odds, God did miracles! When the leaders allowed their people to go astray, punishment came over the whole country. God's principles are no different here in the United States. God blesses the people that serve him. Although our country is suffering from greed and lust of the flesh (desiring things that aren't ours), if we surrender our lives and ambitions to God and ask for His guidance, He will bring victory in His way and time.

We as Christians must be a light by bowing ourselves before God and praying for our country and our leaders and standing up for what God would have us to stand up for. This is the same answer to our personal lives and how to be victorious. The answer is exactly the same! Humble yourself and pray. Seek God's face, and turn back from sinful things in your life. You will hear from God, and He will heal you and heal your land!

Prayer:

"Lord Jesus, this world and the things around me are out of my control. Only You have the power to overcome the problems and evil of this world. Help me to do my part! I humble myself before You, I seek your face and I ask that You show me the areas of my life that are not pleasing to You so that I may turn them over to You and live the right way. I want to hear from You and see You move in my life and in this country. I also pray for all the leaders of our country and that you would bless and lead them along your path. I pray they would humble themselves and seek your direction. Amen."

 **Application Questions:**

1. How deeply are you in prayer for your country?

2. How deeply are you in prayer for your leaders?

3. When is the last time you have humbled yourself before God and sought His face?

4. What is God showing you when you completely surrender and listen?

5. Is there any sin in your life that you need to repent from so that God can move?

6. How often do you pray for revival?

7. Do you look to men or to God for your answers in life?

 **Action Plan:**

Take 10-15 minutes over the next three days to have time alone with God to specifically ask Him to show you any areas of your life in which you are falling short, and write those areas down. Next, read through each one, and ask God to forgive you of these areas of sin. Look to see if these are consistent problem areas for you or if they are infrequent situations. If they are consistent problem areas, then it will require some lifestyle changes and commitments to God's way of living. To accomplish these changes you may want to recruit some help in the form of accountability, coaching, or counseling. If they are infrequent areas, then consider what caused them to happen and what you can put in place to prevent them from occurring again. Ask God (through prayer) to help you, to lead you, and to guide you so that you will live for Him and glorify Him with your life. Also, make it your priority to pray for your leaders at work and at the government level on a daily basis.

35

LOVE WHO?

How well do you do the hard thing – love, pray for and "do good" to your enemies?

Luke 6:35 "But love your enemies, do good to them, and lend to them without expecting to get anything back. Then your reward will be great, and you will be sons of the Most High, because he is kind to the ungrateful and wicked."

If you have been a Christian very long, you know there are some "hard" teachings of Jesus. These were tough to live by when Jesus said them and are tough to live by today. One of those "hard" teachings is found in Luke 6:35. It's tough to pray for someone whom you are at odds with but when Jesus tells us to literally do good to them, that is a real challenge.

A woman who survived a Nazi death camp saw the rest of her family perish there. As a young girl arriving at the camp, a German guard pointed her to stand in one line and the rest of her family in another. Her family's line led to death while her line led to life. This woman later became a Christian and one day spoke about her experience to a group. She stressed forgiveness! After the talk the soldier who pointed her family to the death line came up to shake her hand. He did not recognize her, but she recognized him. She agonized about shaking his hand because of what he did to her loved ones. Finally, through the power of Christ, she grabbed his hand, and immediately a great peace came over her soul!

In another situation a close Christian sister was recently deeply offended by a friend. I saw the hurt and tears, and I also saw her give it all over to the Lord. Later that week her friend asked for a big favor. I saw my Christian sister do something that moved me, and I wasn't sure I could do it. She said "yes" – without hesitation, without malice – with only love. Nothing was said about the incident between the two, but the friend who offended was changed because of unconditional love in response to her destructive actions. Hard? Yes! Eternal? Yes!

Most of us were never in a Nazi concentration camp nor have most of us witnessed harm being done to our families. Hopefully, we never will. However, there are many times we are hurt and offended by others. In order to respond the way Christ wants us to, He must fill our hearts! You must put your burdens on His shoulders by crying out to Him, surrendering to Him, and allowing all vengeance to be His. Allow Christ to flow through you so strongly that only love comes out. As a famous quote says: "Whenever you squeeze something, whatever is inside comes out". The only thing that should come out of us Christians when squeezed is love.

Prayer:

"Lord Jesus, it is hard, very hard, to love those who have hurt me. Please help me in this. My mind wants me to get back or get even, but You want me to love and do good. I see what You did on the cross for me when I was a sinner. Please help me love in that way. Amen"

Application Questions:

1. Who are some of the people you have been at odds with for any reason?

2. Have you forgiven them?

3. Do you pray for blessings in their lives?

4. If they would come to ask you a favor, would you respond in love?

5. What can you do to pray for, love, or even help them today?

6. When you're squeezed for any reason, does the love of God come out or something else?

7. Who do you know (to learn from) who always allows the love of Christ to flow through?

Action Plan:

Think of someone you are at odds with. How long has this situation been gnawing at you? Pray to God to show you what to do next. Are you ready and willing to forgive him or her completely? Many times, if the hurt is deep it can help to write a letter to the offender (but not one that you will send or deliver) describing what happened, how it hurt you, how you feel, and finally that you forgive him or her. Next, burn that letter while you pray, and release that person to Christ. Finally, put that person on your prayer list, and pray for him or her each day, asking from the heart that God will bless and lead this individual to Him in every area. If this is too difficult for you to do right now, continue to pray and ask God to help you and it may be good to seek the support of a Christian counselor.

36 | MOST IMPORTANT

No prayer, no power.

1 John 2:17 "The world and its desires pass away, but whoever does the will of God lives forever."

What is the most important thing in your life? Most Christians would answer by saying something like "a relationship with Jesus" or "living for Christ". The main theme would be "following God".

I thought of my own answer to that question then asked myself, "Would someone else looking at my life say Christ is my priority?' More importantly, does God see it that way? I thought I was doing pretty well living a godly life. I go to church, I have a small group meeting each week, I serve in the church, and I do my daily devotions. Not bad, or so I thought, until God hit me over the head with a spiritual 2 x 4.

David Yonggi Cho pastors the largest Protestant church in the world in Seoul, South Korea (with over 750,000 members). I read an article about an interview he had with another pastor from the United States. The U.S. Pastor asked Cho how he stays fresh in the ministry. His answer was simple. He said when he started his ministry he spent five hours every day in prayer and now spends three hours per day. He believes most American pastors work very hard but lack the "determination to pray things through. No prayer power!" He continued by saying most people do not know the real importance of prayer.

God connected this way of thinking for me with a video I watched several months before about the greatest revival that has ever hit the United States, called the "Azusa Street Revival." This revival happened just over 100 years ago and started with one man praying for 5 hours per day. Since its occurrence, it has impacted more than 100,000,000 people worldwide.

Every great act of God in a society, country, town, or in your life must be preceded by prayer. Saying your top priority is your relationship with God, but not spending time with Him is a contradiction. You may not be able to pray five, three, or even one hour per day right now, but make a commitment to yourself and to God about how much time you will spend with Him in prayer, even if it's 10 minutes a day. Then do it. When you pray, be real with your Father: open your heart and listen to what He shows you. Make sure the top priority in your life is the same as what you say it is.

Prayer:

"Lord Jesus, You showed me how to walk with the Father by doing it Yourself. Help me to do the same. I desire to hear You, to know You, to walk with You. Help my priorities line up with what I say they are. Help me to set aside time to be with You, to listen to You speak to me, Lord! Amen."

Application Questions:

1. How much time are you really spending with God?

2. Could you say that you truly walk with God on a daily basis?

3. What do you need to pray through until you get God's answer?

4. What is the longest time you have ever spent in prayer?

5. When is the last time you took at least 10 minutes just to listen to God?

6. What is your biggest challenge with prayer?

7. What can you do to overcome any challenges you have with your prayer life?

Action Plan:

For one week spend 10 minutes per day listening in quietness for God to speak to you. It may take some work to quiet your mind if you're not used to it. Here are some tips that can help you if your mind starts to wander and you begin to think about things you need to get done or other things about your daily life. Keep a note pad handy to jot the worldly thoughts down so you can come back to them later, but move forward in prayer. Also, you can think of a Bible verse or praise and worship lyric that focuses your mind on Christ. One of my favorite lyrics is from Rebecca St James: it says, "Speak to me, Lord, for Your child is here listening." Finally, write down in your journal or on paper what God reveals to you.

37 YOU'RE ASKING FOR IT

God will give what you ask if it's according to His will, but what if it's according to your will?

James 5:16 "Therefore confess your sins to each other and pray for each other so that you may be healed. The prayer of a righteous person is powerful and effective."

Imagine you have a five-year-old son who somehow finds a box of matches. You immediately take them away. He kicks, screams, and yells because he wants those matches – they are his! He feels that he found them, and he deserves them! At five years old he may have no idea about the purpose of those little wooden sticks. Of course when the matches are used for the right purpose, they can light a furnace, light a stove, and do other powerful things. That same box of matches can also be destructive. You, as the parent, know the good purpose; the five year old does not.

I'll never forget, when I was a child, our family was camping in the forest, and somehow I found a box of matches. On a nearby tree I was trying to light one of them with another little friend. My mom (and Smokey the Bear) nearly had a heart attack when she found me with the matches.

In areas of our lives we are the same as that child. We think we have wisdom and maturity, but many times we don't. Jesus knew this. In Hebrews 10:7 He says, "I have come to do your will, Oh God." Then, before going to the cross, He said, "Your will, not mine, be done."

All that Jesus did (save mankind, fulfill prophesies, heal the sick, etc.) was what the Father directed him to do. Jesus' purpose was to follow God the Father's purposes. The key for us is to pray, as Jesus prayed. We will face many challenges, situations, people, and problems in life. The "matches" are the decisions we make responding to situations. Jesus prayed what was on His heart yet did not demand His will be done. He committed to following the Father's will.

We don't have perspective on life the way God does. We have to believe He knows best and ask Him to lead our choices to best glorify Him. Pray that God's will be done, and He will give you strength and wisdom to follow. "The prayer of a righteous man (or woman) avails much."

1 John 5:14–15 says "This is the confidence we have in approaching God: that if we ask anything according to his will, He hears us. And if we know that He hears us – whatever we ask – we know that we have what we asked of him." You can always ask to keep the matches (your "will" and "plan"), and if God has a purpose for those in your life, He will let you keep them. If God does not want you to have them, be willing to give up the matches because they could be destructive. God always has the best plan for your life.

Prayer:
"Lord Jesus, thank You for showing me how to pray and how to live. Help me to do what You have done by knowing and submitting to the Father's will. Amen."

Application Questions:

1. How righteous (in right standing with God) of a life do you live?

2. Do you seek to know God's will?

3. How often do you pray asking for God's will (as compared to your own)?

4. How willing are you to follow God's will if it does not agree with yours?

5. Do you pray "Your will, not my will be done"?

6. What do you feel is your greatest purpose on this earth?

7. Who do you have as a role model who follows God's will?

Action Plan:

How important do you view the daily decisions in your life? If you view your decisions as powerful "matches" to be used for amazing kingdom purposes, God will lead you to great victory in life. If you view them as something to be taken very lightly and to only have fun with (by trying to strike them on forest trees), you will experience turmoil and possible destruction in life. Think about some of the decisions you make on a daily basis. Do you ask Jesus for direction, and do you think through your decisions, or are you striking your matches dangerously? Also think about the important decisions in life (career changes, marriage, moving, and others) and how you approach those decisions. The next step to take is to picture matches in your hand this week as you make a decision. Before you light one, think about what you're doing, why you're doing it and most importantly – what would Jesus have you do.

38

ON GUARD!

You are God's soldier fighting in a glorious battle that must be taken seriously!

1 Peter 5:8 "Be alert and of sober mind. Your enemy the devil prowls around like a roaring lion looking for someone to devour."

Several years ago a wild boar was spotted roaming around our condo development. If you're not familiar with these animals, they can be extremely mean and aggressive, especially if startled. If you're not careful around one, you could end up seriously hurt. I'm not much of a trapper, so Claudia and I mostly stayed inside until we knew it had been caught. However, I did need to go out a couple times, so I prepared. I was cautious about my surroundings, paid attention to details, and planned my route with the shortest distances to where I was going.

Imagine that were you, and instead of a wild boar, it was an actual lion in your neighborhood that was known for hunting down people. Imagine also that you had to go outside regularly knowing this animal was prowling around. How would you prepare and what would you do?

Although I pray this situation never happens to you in the physical world, this "lion on the loose" is always the case in the spiritual world according to 1 Peter 5. Against this lion, Satan, the walls of your house or any other building will not protect you. It is important for you as a child of God to take this seriously – as if your life depended on it, because it does. Since we don't see the spiritual world, it is easy to take it for granted, but the foundation of our physical world is based on it. Therefore, you need to know your enemy, how he operates, and how to defend against him.

The Bible has strong images of who God is, who Satan is, and who we are. It's amazing to study the many incredible names for God (Prince of Peace, Mighty Warrior, great I Am, The Rock, and many more). We can stand on His promise that He will be all these things in our lives. He also has many names for us – lambs, children, sheep, His bride, etc. Then there is our enemy, Satan, whom He describes as deceiver, prince of the air, and liar, as well as lion.

We are already in this battle with an intense and cunning adversary. You need to prepare, to plan, and to fight spiritually. This lion attacks your mind first and brings fear, doubt, temptation, and many evil things! You are a soldier of God, so put on your armor every day (Ephesians 6:10–18). Be self-controlled and alert. Take captive your thoughts for Christ by memorizing scripture and standing firm on the truth. You will have incredible victory every day over the one trying to destroy you and will be able to help others as well! The great news is, we win!

Prayer:

"Lord Jesus, I realize I alone am no match for this battle I am in. I could not defeat an aggressive lion without weapons, strategy, or strength. You are all those things and more in my life. Help me to daily spend time with You and to put on my armor for battle. Amen."

Application Questions:

1. How seriously do you take this daily battle that you are in against Satan?

2. How many days per week do you go into battle without your armor on?

3. Are you alert to the deceptions of Satan in your life?

4. Are you self-controlled enough to keep Satan from getting a foothold in your life?

5. In what areas of your life are you spiritually strong in your battle against Satan?

6. In what areas of your life are you spiritually weak?

7. Are you taking captive every thought according to the knowledge of Christ Jesus?

Action Plan:

If you really knew a physical battle was coming and you had to be in it, I am sure you would take it seriously. Think about the five top things you would do to prepare for this battle. Your list may include preparing in the following ways: mentally, physically, strategically, and spiritually. Thankfully, for most of us, we will not have to face this type of physical battle, but today and every day we do face a spiritual battle. Unfortunately, many times we are unprepared. So now consider those five areas on your list and how you can prepare similarly for your battle against Satan. Also, read Ephesians 6:10–18 to get some ideas from God's Word about how we should prepare for battle. List what you need to change in your life to take this battle seriously and to fight the good fight against the enemy. Finally, list where and when you will start putting these changes into effect, and recruit a fellow "soldier" or two to help you.

39 — HOW HARD COULD IT REALLY BE?

Living a righteous life is simple – when you submit all your thoughts to God!

2 Corinthians 10:5 "Take captive every thought and make it obedient to Christ."

Doesn't life seem as if it should be so simple? We read the Bible and God tells us how to live, then we think to ourselves – "Yeah, I can do that!" Then, after about two minutes, that feeling goes away as tests, trials, tribulations, temptations, and other life challenges come our way. As we step back into the world from our time with God, we realize it's not so easy. But then again, Christ told us it would be a challenge. It wasn't easy for Him either, but it was well worth it.

Many times it is quite hard to put into daily life even the simple things God tells us to do. 2 Corinthians 10:5 is intense! God commands us to take our own thoughts captive. This is hard enough to do with one thought, but He wants us to do this with every thought. If that weren't tough enough, we then have to make each thought obey God's Word.

Our thoughts generally come from one of three sources: God, Satan, or ourselves – only one of which is worth having. God gives us free will to choose what we want to think about, which then determines our actions. That is where the danger lies. There is an evil force with an evil agenda that is really good at imposing it on our thoughts. He knows us better than we know ourselves! All he has to do at a weak time in our lives is present a way to get revenge, a cigarette, a beautiful woman, lots of money, a bottle of alcohol, material things, or whatever else will lead our minds down a path to destruction.

The other force that can lead to bondage is our own desire. This usually comes from emotions that our eyes, ears, or other senses play on. It gets us thinking about and longing for something that is not at all God's plan. What attracts us in the physical world many times does not agree with God's perfect plan.

Here is the key – at the point when a thought first enters our mind is most critical. Right then we have a choice regarding how we will proceed. We can either feed what is false or take the thought captive according to God's truth. In order to do this we must study God's Word through daily devotion time. Learn and know God's Word by memorizing scripture. Then, most importantly, use God's Word by quoting scripture against any evil thought that Satan planted in your mind.

Prayer:

"Lord Jesus, my biggest battle goes on within my own mind. Help me realize what I am harboring there, and show me what does not agree with Your Word. Help me take captive wrong thoughts as soon as they enter my mind so I may not become obedient to them, but only to You. Help me love You and others in all I think, say, and do. In Jesus name I pray, Amen!"

Application Questions:

1. How quickly do you realize when your thought is not pure, productive, or Godly?

2. How much time do you spend daily reading God's Word?

3. How many scriptures do you have memorized?

4. How well do you stand up against wrong thoughts by using God's Word?

5. How quickly do you take captive a wrong thought and remove it?

6. In what areas of life do you need to search for and memorize God's promises?

7. How much time do you spend meditating on scripture, God's truth, and Christ Himself?

Action Plan:

Take three situations over the next couple days to try this. When a thought comes to your mind, seemingly out of nowhere, before acting on it or throwing it out, take a minute to review the idea. Consider where that thought came from and what may have triggered it. Is it a Godly thought, evil thought, or seemingly neither? Consider what acting on that thought would lead to. Now, think about what you were doing when the thought entered your mind. Were you in the middle of something Godly, ungodly, or neutral at that time? Next, you have to do something with the idea. If it is from God, pray for His guidance and direction, then pursue His plan. If it is just a miscellaneous idea or an evil one, let it go and turn your attention to something holy, like a scripture, worship lyrics, etc. It is very important to realize that catching a thought when it first enters our minds is most critical. Learn to recognize immediately where the inspiration is coming from so you can discard it and move on, or act in faith if it's God's direction.

40 YOUR GREATEST FAN

What's your "fan project" that, if God turned the power on to it right now, could be destructive?

Ecclesiastes 3:1 "There's a time for everything and a season for every activity under the heavens."

Several months ago I was helping my father-in-law with a home-improvement project. The project was installing several ceiling fans in his home, and because I had some experience with it, I thought I could help. If you've ever put up a ceiling fan, you know that it's not a 10 minute project and there are multiple parts to assemble. At one point, when you have the bulk of the fan assembled on the floor, you have to lift it up and hold it there to connect the electrical wires.

At one point I was on top of a ladder holding the base of the fan with my left hand and the electrical wires with my right. Just then my wife walked in and asked me one of the most alarming questions I have ever heard. "Did anyone turn off the electricity?" Immediately I turned pale and felt the hair on my arms stand up (wondering if I was being electrocuted). I quickly turned to my father-in-law, while brilliantly still holding the wires, just in time to hear him say "NO". At that point I think I had a mild heart attack! He said, "I didn't cut the main switch but the switch on the wall is off." After some deep breaths, I recovered and helped finish the project.

A little while later, while putting up another ceiling fan (I let my father-in-law hold the wires on), I was thinking of the previous situation. If the power had actually been on, what would have happened? At minimum, I would have been shocked! I could have been hurt badly, possibly even killed. Then I realized, in spiritual terms, there are many projects in my life that God has me working on, but I want results right now. I think I am done with the project, yet I don't realize that if God "turned on the power" right now, it could cause much harm, even devastation.

Before we put the ceiling fan together, we could see the picture on the box of what it would look like, and we would think about how beautiful it would be in the room. When we opened the box, we found a bunch of parts. A little while later we could still see the "vision" on the box, but now we had a hole in the ceiling with portions of a fan put together on the floor. Today all of the fans look nice, and we lived through it.

Maybe God has given you a vision and all you are seeing are the parts on the floor. Even worse, maybe you just see a hole in the ceiling and partially put-together "stuff" in your life. I really encourage you to keep your eyes on Jesus, the dream giver. Keep pursuing what He calls you to. Remember, if He turned the power on right now, it could be the worst thing to ever happen. Finish the plan – He is building something beautiful in you!

Prayer:
"Lord, Jesus, thank You for loving me. Thank You for leading me. Thank You for watching over me. I trust You with every area of my life. Help me just to listen and follow You. Amen."

Application Questions:

1. What is a "fan project" in your life?

2. How long have you been working on and waiting for this vision?

3. What are the pieces and parts you see around you?

4. Can you still see the "picture on the box" of what God has shown you?

5. What is the "hole in the ceiling" related to you vision or goal?

6. Are you willing to work on whatever He calls you to until it's time for electricity?

7. Do you trust God with every area of your life right now – including this vision?

Action Plan:

It can be a challenge in our lives to wait for God's plan to come together. However, this is where He grows and changes us if we let Him. It is important to confirm that your vision is from God, so spend some time to pray and confirm what you think you want is actually from Him and not from you. If it is not from Christ, let it go, and move on. If it is from God, it's still important to let it go by turning it over to Him. Turn this vision or dream over to Him by surrendering to His will, His plan, and His timing. Don't set your own plan to try and make it happen. Finally, what does God want you doing today? If it is working on areas of this vision, then go for it and give it your best. If not, do what God calls you to today and trust that in the right time that "fan project" will be complete and beautiful with the power turned on at just the right time. Remember, the greatest goal we can achieve each day is to say, "Well done good and faithful servant!"

41 HOW TO GROW UP – SPIRITUALLY!

Until you mature spiritually, you cannot move to the higher level.

Hebrews 5:12-14 "In fact, though by this time you ought to be teachers, you need someone to teach you the elementary truths of God's word all over again. You need milk, not solid food! Anyone who lives on milk, being still an infant, is not acquainted with the teaching about righteousness. But solid food is for the mature, who by constant use have trained themselves to distinguish good from evil."

Imagine a young child that you are trying to teach how to play basketball. You buy him a little Nerf hoop that stands four feet tall, and you show him the "granny shot". You know that one, where you bring the ball back between your legs and with both arms hoist the ball up into the air and hope to hit something (no offense to Granny's reading this who do shoot that way).

Imagine you keep playing with the child – the same ball, the same net, and the same height – for weeks and months, and he gets really good. Later you raise the hoop. The child keeps playing and practicing until he is good at that level too. Next you buy a real hoop, but you lower it to 6 feet and give the child a smaller plastic ball to try. What a shock. He's not as good as he was on the other hoop, but once he perfects the scenario, you give him the real ball. Again it's like starting over but after some time he gets good. Now you show him the overhead shot. Everything in his basketball career is now a mess; he can't seem to do anything right. After lots of practice, he gets the ball into the basket consistently, and then you raise the hoop to normal height. After some time, the boy is now shooting overhand, with a real ball on a real hoop. He has grown and matured.

When you first accept Christ, is it like the child learning basketball for the very first time. It's the basics. You're just trying to learn about love, about God, and about truth. It's exciting and fun. Soon, though, you realize you have the basics down, but now the game changes. You are challenged with temptations, trials, and hard things in life, and it's not so fun. You have to apply what you've learned in the Bible. You now go through what seems like "never-ending practice" with that co-worker who seems evil or that sin you just can't beat.

Before God can "raise the hoop," you have to learn more about love, truth, and the spiritual disciplines right where you are. You have to practice in the middle of the problem. The ball may have been changed on you or the hoop raised, but the purpose is still the same. Grow close to God, learn His truths, stand upon his word, and, most importantly, learn to love. Put the ball in the hoop. Imagine the struggle men and women like Billy Graham, Mother Theresa, and other "spiritual giants" must have faced in learning to grow spiritually. We are no different. Don't forget about learning to grow where you are, and mature spiritually to gain faith and obedience.

Prayer:
"Lord Jesus, help me not to stay stagnant but to grow in my spiritual walk with You. Amen!"

 **Application Questions:**

1. How much have you matured spiritually since you gave your life over to Christ?

2. How much do you want to mature spiritually from where you are right now?

3. Why do you want to grow in spiritual maturity?

4. Are you willing to go through challenges and stretching from God to mature?

5. What obstacles have held you back from maturing spiritually?

6. What is the first thing you need to work on spiritually right now to grow?

7. Whom do you know that is more spiritually mature who can mentor you?

Action Plan:

Think about the child learning to shoot a basketball, and compare his growth with your spiritual maturity. Are you at stage one, where you have just become a Christian, and are trying to understand all this, or would you say you have been a Christian for a while and attend church but haven't grown into great faith yet? Maybe you are at the stage where you've been learning, working, and applying godly principles but don't feel you understand the deep things of God. Or you may consider yourself to be a mature Christian who is well versed in Bible theology, walks by faith through life's trials, and stands on God's Word through all situations. No matter what stage you are in, there are still ways God wants to grow you. The next question is, are you really willing to mature and grow, even if the process stretches you from the core? If your answer is "Yes," then tell Jesus your desire to grow with Him. Begin to study and learn more of the Bible, and learn from other mature believers. If your answer is "no," ask God to reveal to you why you don't have a desire to grow up in the faith.

42

NOT SO BEAUTIFUL

Just because we think something is good for us doesn't mean it is!

1 John 5:14 "And this is the confidence that we have in Him, that if we ask anything according to His will, he hears us."

My wife and I have two "furry children" named Bonita and Bella. Both names mean "beautiful" in different languages (obviously to avoid doggie jealousy). The older sister, Bo, loves to eat! We can tell when she overeats because her belly grows quite obviously. This puts more pressure on her hips, so then she doesn't walk as easily, and she gets tired quickly. When we go for daily walks after she eats too much, she doesn't have the energy to do the 1.5 mile loop very well. Sound familiar to anyone?

We used to put a cup of dog food in one bowl for the dogs to share. Unfortunately, they didn't. Bella takes her time eating while Bo devours food like a garbage disposal. Bella stayed skinny and Bo gained weight. We have since changed our strategy; We now give Bella half a cup and put Bonita in her cage with her portion. Bo doesn't come out until Bella is done. Now Bella seems to torture her sister by eating even slower while Bonita watches and suffers.

Here is the principle we all can learn from: It's not wrong for Bonita to want food; she needs it to live. However, it is wrong for her to eat all that she wants just to fill her cravings. This would lead to poor health and an immobile life. As her owners, we realize she has this problem controlling her eating, so we only feed her what she needs. She has a beautiful coat and frame and lots of energy. If we gave her all the food she really wanted she would be in trouble and not even know it.

How often do we do this in our spiritual lives? We know what we want. We think we know what's good for us, but we don't know what God does. Some of the things we really want in life could be our downfall, or someone else's, if God gave them to us. From our perspective, it seems as if He tortures us as we watch someone else with more money or talent or you name it!

1 John 5 clearly explains that we need to pray for God's will, desires, and timing for our lives! When we get in our minds what we think is best and expect only that, we are setting ourselves up for major disappointment. God wants you to ask Him to supply your needs, and then trust Him to do it. We need to ask God to change our hearts in all areas that we have wrong ambitions and for Him to lead us in the way we should go. He will give you all you need. If He gives additional blessings to you, then great, but if He doesn't – it's the best thing for your life.

Prayer:

"Lord, Jesus, it is so easy in this world to want all the things in it. Please help me realize all these things I think I want or need may not be what You want. My heart is open! Perform Your spiritual surgery to make me whole and new every day by desiring what you desire. Amen."

Application Questions:

1. Are you asking God for things according to His will or yours?

2. What things in life could pull you away from God if you had too much of them?

3. What do you need to ask for today from God to meet your needs?

4. What do you need to ask for today to supply the needs of those around you?

5. How can you know if you are praying according to God's will?

6. If God doesn't answer your prayer the way you want, how will you respond?

7. Who is a good prayer partner for you that will help you pray according to God's will?

Action Plan:

The action step to apply here is very powerful and can be life changing. During your next quiet time with God, think about all the things in your life God has blessed you with. If you are having a hard time with this, start with the basics, such as food for the day, a friend or family member, a roof over your head, even having the ability to read this book. As you think of these things God has given you in areas related to your health, career, finances, abilities, relationships, and other key areas, express your thanks to Him for them. You can do this by praying, writing it down, or even telling someone else. Next, go through each of these areas you are thankful for, and offer them back up to God. In other words, proclaiming those things are His and He can do with them whatever He wants. Really turn these things over to Christ; they are His anyway. Offer everything you have for His purpose, including giving it away if He leads you to.

43 | THEN WHAT?

We spend time, money, and energy to focus on goals, but when we reach them – Then what?

Matthew 6:19–20 "Do not store up for yourselves treasures on earth, where moths and vermin destroy, and where thieves break in and steal. But store up for yourselves treasures in heaven, where moths and vermin do not destroy, and where thieves do not break in and steal."

There was a busy American businessman taking a needed vacation at a Mexican beach resort. Unfortunately, he couldn't leave work at home. While taking a business call on his cell phone at a local restaurant, he noticed a fisherman finishing his day by lunchtime for the third day in a row. The fisherman pulled his boat to shore, sold most of his catch, then went to be with his family for the afternoon, just like every other day. Later at night he returned to have some food and fun with friends, then went home for a good night's rest.

The businessman decided to help the talented fisherman. He told the fisherman he had a great business idea. He said if you start fishing the full day, you can catch three times the amount of fish. "Then what?" asked the fisherman. Then you can take the extra money and buy another boat and hire another fisherman. "Then what?" he asked. Then you have double the capacity and profits to buy more fishing boats. "Then what?" replied the fisherman. Soon you have a fleet of boats, a thriving business, and lots of profit. "Then what?" Well, then you could sell your company to make a big profit. "And then what?" asked the confused fisherman. Well, then you could do whatever you wanted to do, like go fishing in the morning, spend time with your family through the afternoon, and hang with friends at night.

The moral here is not to move to Mexico and buy a fishing boat – although it's tempting. The real key is to realize that things can occupy our lives, but choosing the right ones to dedicate time and energy to is most important. We need to live life in the process of achieving our goals. We are not to pursue wealth and position while leaving others behind. It's not biblical. Even having a ministry that helps others and forsakes loved ones is wrong.

Work and work hard at the things God has called you to do and in the areas He has gifted you. At the same time live life today and everyday by laughing, enjoying others, sharing the love of Jesus, and expressing that love to those God has put around you. We are not guaranteed another day on this earth, and God has given us a life to live and amazing people to love today. If you store up material treasures and accomplishments, they will benefit you for a few years. If you store up eternal treasures, those people will join you in heaven – and thank you for eternity!

Prayer:

"Lord Jesus, help me to have balance in my life just as You did when you walked the face of the earth. Help me to see You all day long, to apply myself to be productive in this world, to earn the respect of others so they may listen to what You have done in my life and follow you. Help me also to enjoy my life and truly live it today. Amen"

Application Questions:

1. Are you working hard to fulfill God's dream yet forgetting to live life?

2. How much time are you dedicating per day to your closest loved ones?

3. Are you just "playing around" and not taking life seriously?

4. Are you taking life so seriously that you have no play time to enjoy it?

5. How can you make sure to take time to laugh today?

6. If you were given six months to live, how would your priorities change?

7. What would your closest family and friends say your priorities are from watching you?

Action Plan:

Your goal here is to take the next 24 hours and write down how you spend your time. Break it down into 15 or 30 minute blocks. A tip in doing this is to keep with you whatever you are using to record this (your planner, computer, or notebook) all day. Next, look over how you spent your time. Is it what you thought it would be? Is it what you want it to be? Compare this to your typical day to see if this is normal for you. Now think of the fisherman who not only worked hard and provided for his family, but also spent daily time with them and had balance. List up to three areas you need to change to have more balance in life. Determine what area you want to make a change in first (you may ask friends or family for ideas); then set up a plan with a deadline to make the change. This is your mission – if you choose to accept it. Thankfully, this book will not self-destruct in 10 seconds.

44 UNITY

If you keep your eyes on your Leader, everything will flow in excellent unity.

Colossians 3:1–4 "Since, then, you have been raised with Christ, set your hearts on things above, where Christ is, seated at the right hand of God. Set your minds on things above, not on earthly things. For you died, and your life is now hidden with Christ in God. When Christ, who is your life, appears, then you also will appear with him in glory."

A few years back I had the distinct privilege of hearing one of the nation's best choirs perform live. They came from Kentucky Christian University and had just performed in major venues including Carnegie Hall and an international choir festival held in Cuba. Their performance was so moving that they brought the crowd to tears several times during their performance (which is the opposite reason I bring people to tears when I sing).

During the encore performance my wife and I stood up front with the prayer team. From the front of the stage I got a totally different view of the performance. I could now see the choir close up. Even more remarkable was to watch the conductor's face and actions as he led the performance. He had amazing intensity, passion, and coordination as nearly 80 talented college students followed his every command. I realized that the beautiful sound I was seeing and hearing from the choir was in direct reflection to the actions of the conductor.

Without a conductor passionately leading the songs, teaching the choir to sing in harmony, seeing the vision of a coordinated performance, and making the commitment to fulfill a purpose of excellence, there would have just been a large group of incredibly skilled singers out of sync, out of harmony, and in chaos on stage. God revealed to me that each member of that choir closely focused on the conductor. They followed his words, his mannerisms, his directions and especially his passion. They followed his lead to a superb performance.

God then put the thought in my mind – What if we all focused on Christ in our daily lives the way this choir focused on their conductor? Imagine what the unity of the spirit would produce in our homes, our workplaces, and our churches if we were totally in one accord with Christ. Imagine what it would be like if we directed our personal lives to use our skills and talents to full potential by willingly focusing on every passionate leading of Jesus Christ. The accounts we read about in the book of Acts would be reborn. There would be a true community where each other's needs would be taken care of by his brother and sister in Christ. Look intently at your "life conductor's" face. Follow His lead, and watch what the unity of the spirit will produce.

Prayer:

"Lord Jesus, I pray that You be my life's conductor – every day and in every way. Help me to see You with absolute clarity and reflect You in all areas of my life. All the skills, talents and abilities were given by You to me, so help me use them in unison with other brothers and sisters around me. Help me to follow You today, and let not my will be done, but only Yours. Amen."

Application Questions:

1. Who is the real conductor for your life right now?

2. How well are you doing your part to focus fully and intently on God and his leading?

3. What is your biggest obstacle to focusing fully on God?

4. How can you improve your focus on Jesus?

5. What does "being in unison" mean to you?

6. In what areas of your life are you working in unison with other believers?

7. In what areas of life do you feel out of sync with God or other Christians?

Action Plan:

To complete this Action Plan, you must look within yourself. What conductor does your heart follow on a moment-by-moment and day-by-day basis? Take a minute to think about this. To answer "Jesus" would mean that you pray about all things during the day and that you sense His Spirit all the time. It means you also have the passion for what His passion is, and you desire to follow His every move. If this is your daily life – excellent! Not many believers can say it is. Most of us fall short. If you are walking this closely with Christ, your next best step is to ask God to show you someone who needs a good mentor. For the rest of us striving to keep Jesus always at the forefront, think back to the time you walked closest with Christ. What did you do differently, think differently, or have in place as a habit to help you stay in tune? What do you need to change to live that way again? If you get back to basics, you will see and follow the conductor's (God's) every movement.

45

TOP PRIORITY

Be ready and sensitive to the Holy Spirit – the Great Commission is right in front of you.

Matthew 28:18–20 "Then Jesus came to them and said, 'All authority in heaven and on earth has been given to me. Therefore go and make disciples of all nations, baptizing them in the name of the Father and of the Son and of the Holy Spirit, and teaching them to obey everything I have commanded you. And surely I am with you always, to the very end of the age.'"

One day, while mountain bike riding with my brother-in-law, we took a short break at a turn off and met a man named Woody. Woody was really into mountain biking and is on the trails three or more times a week. As we talked, he said his girlfriend always asks him to go to church on Sundays, but he doesn't want to. He then said he doesn't need to spend two hours in a stuffy room listening to someone talk when he can be out in God's creation and experience Him.

This was a perfect open door for us to witness to Woody, who obviously was turned off by church. In talking with him more, it seemed he had been rejected a lot by society because of his physical appearance, and he was able to break away from the world by being alone on the trails. I knew this was the perfect time to witness to him. I searched for the right words to say during 20 seconds (which seemed like 20 minutes) of complete silence. Then Woody said "I'll see you guys later" and rode off. My heart sank! I realized I missed it – the purpose I am on this earth for – to help save a lost soul. I went blank for words. To me, this is the worst feeling for a Christian can have.

It is easy for any of us to get preoccupied or even consumed with all that's happening around us in this world. We can easily forget the priorities Jesus gave us. The first priority is the Great Commandment to love God with all of our being and love our neighbors as ourselves. Living this commandment is a challenge when so many things on this earth call for our attention.

If we are not living our lives based on the Great Commandment, it becomes almost impossible to fulfill the Great Commission, which is what Jesus said in Matthew 28:18–20. We can do so many great things in the world, but if we don't make the Great Commandment and Great Commission our priority, it is all a waste. I have been praying for Woody and hoping to meet up with him again one day. More importantly, I pray he will surrender his heart and his hurts to our Lord Jesus Christ. We all need to be ready, willing, and able to share the good news. Pray for the Holy Spirit to give you the words and boldness at all times to speak the gospel of Jesus to this lost and dying world – it's what the world needs.

Prayer:

"Lord Jesus, I know I am only on this earth for a short time. Help me to love You more deeply than ever before with all that is within me. Also, I ask that You guide me every minute of every day to be a witness to those around me and to share the good news of Your salvation. I am Your child! Amen."

Application Questions:

1. What would your closest friend say your life purpose is (from watching your life)?

2. If I asked your non-Christian friends if you told them about Jesus, what would they say?

3. What will you commit to today regarding living the Great Commandment?

4. What will you commit to today regarding sharing Christ with others?

5. Is there anyone Jesus has been leading you to witness to, and you have been avoiding it?

6. Who do you know that is living for Christ and witnessing to others?

7. What can you learn from those Godly and Christ sharing people?

Action Plan:

Make a list of five people in your life that do not know Christ. These could be family, friends, coworkers, neighbors, or anyone else God puts on your heart. How many of these, if any, have you shared the Good News with? Over the next five weeks, schedule a time to meet with or talk with these individuals. It could be a lunch outing, a special event, or a simple phone call. The purpose is not specifically to share the gospel; the purpose is to pray that the Holy Spirit will lead you in your conversation, and if it is time to share the gospel, then do so. The other important reason to do this is to simply keep in touch and let the other person know you care and want to have a relationship. You can be praying for them until you meet and offer to pray for them at the end of your meeting. Keep in mind, their mindset and responses are out of your control. What is in your control is the ability to reach out to them and to pray for them. If you want to read a good book on this subject, pick up a copy of Walk Across the Room by Bill Hybels.

46 WAKE UP

Live each day as if it were your last, because it just might be.

2 Corinthians 4:16–18 "Therefore we do not lose heart. Though outwardly we are wasting away, yet inwardly we are being renewed day by day. For our light and momentary troubles are achieving for us an eternal glory that far outweighs them all. So we fix our eyes not on what is seen, but on what is unseen, since what is seen is temporary, but what is unseen is eternal."

As I woke up today, I realized something – "I woke up today". As odd as this may sound, it is really quite profound. By me finding myself here again on planet earth, it means God wants me to be here another day. There will come a day that will be my last on this earth. No one knows when that is except God himself, but he has a purpose for me being here right now – today. Whether everything is rosy and cheerful in my perspective, or if today is a big struggle and I would rather be home with Jesus, there is a purpose! The same is true for each of us each day we wake up on this earth.

I am reminded of a young man from church who had lost his 43-year-old father. To everyone but God, it was unexpected and a shock. Most things in life you cannot choose – such as when or where you're born, your culture, others actions, or even circumstances in the world around us. However, the most important thing in your life you can choose is your thoughts. Proverbs 23:7 says, "For as he thinketh within himself, so is he." (AMS Bible version). What you choose to think about determines whom you choose to become. Your thoughts determine your actions, and your actions determine your outcomes. God has given you free will and allowed you to choose your path, but keep in mind your path does not start with your actions; it starts in your heart and mind, which then guides your actions.

Choose the right life by choosing the right thoughts. Think upon the Lord! In Philippians 4, God directs us on how to focus our thoughts on the things that are true, noble, right, pure, lovely, acceptable, praiseworthy, and excellent. This is not easy in this evil world, but God has you here today for a purpose, and only by keeping your mind on Him can you fulfill it.

He also directs us to have the same attitude as Christ. This means to rejoice, be positive and to refuse to think or believe contrary to God's Word and promises. Be careful to input only the godly things into your mind. Choose to live life, not sit and worry about it!

Prayer:

"Lord Jesus, I realize I am here for a reason today. Help me forget about the worries of yesterday and trust by growing into a deeper love with You right now. Help me live by choosing the higher life of Your calling. I want to set my mind upon You and the things of You. Help me take captive every thought and make it obedient to You so I may know Your will and follow You always. Thank You for Your love. Amen."

 **Application Questions:**

1. Are your daily thoughts negative or positive?

2. How do you renew your mind daily?

3. How often during the day do you stop, pray, and get transformed by renewing your mind?

4. Do you ask Jesus how He can fulfill His plan in your life and be a blessing to others?

5. God has chosen you to be here another day. What attitude will you face this day with?

6. Will you dedicate yourself to being all God planned for you?

7. Whom do you know that lives life to the fullest every day and how can you learn from them?

 **Action Plan:**

Take a minute to really review this list from Philippians 4 regarding how God directs us to think and focus our minds. We are to set our minds on things that are true, noble, right, pure, lovely, acceptable, praiseworthy, and excellent. Now think about this past week and the people you hung around. Did you hear and talk about things that agreed with these principles or was it off track? Think about the last movie or TV show you watched and how it compared to the thinking that glorifies God. What are the lyrics to the recent songs you listened too?

Even more direct for us in this generation is the following question: What were the websites and internet information you looked at this past week? What you put into your mind directs your thinking. If you think right, you act right. What do you need to put into and/or take out of your life to continually think upon things that are true, noble, right, pure, lovely, acceptable, praiseworthy, and excellent and not all the other junk of this world?

47 SIGNIFICANT

The significance of a person is not defined by creation but by the Creator.

Ephesians 2:10 "For we are God's workmanship, created in Christ Jesus to do good works, which God prepared in advance for us to do."

A very strange thing occurred to me one day while in a church service. As I sat listening to the message regarding the importance of leaving a legacy, a thought came to my mind that there are some people who may never have a chance to leave a legacy, much less a lasting impression on the minds of others. These are people born into captivity, poverty, and poor societies. It may feel to them that their lives are insignificant and even purposeless.

An image then came to my mind of a large tree planted in a wooded area. I asked the Lord what it meant. He revealed to me the apparent insignificance an individual tree has in the middle of a forest with so many other trees around. That one tree could go through its whole existence seemingly providing very little to the earth and mankind. But even that tree has a purpose. God showed me that for the person who owns that wooded area, that one tree provides many things, like beauty, shade and an ecosystem. Even more important for that owner and all the animals around that have breath, is the extremely important oxygen provided by that one tree.

Most of us are not TV stars, Rock stars, or professional athletes. In America nowadays a person's importance is defined by how much he or she is in the lime light and well known. The truth is that no matter how insignificant life, or even certain days, might seem to you, they mean everything to the Creator! To God you are like that tree providing oxygen for human life. By being the person he made you to be through loving him and others around you (even the unlovable), He has pleasure in your very existence.

There is a purpose and reason for your being here on this earth. It does not matter what man thinks; it matters what God thinks. Ask Jesus to use you every day for His purpose and He will. Many days it may not look or feel this way in your daily life, but be sensitive to the Spirit and following His prompting. He is using you. It may be through your smile, a kind word you said, or a way you handle a situation. Your life will speak louder than words if you follow Jesus, and your existence will be like oxygen to the world around you. Even if your circumstances are not how you want them to be, glorify God with who he made you to be. Fulfill your purpose today and "Bloom where you are planted."

Prayer:

"Lord Jesus, sometimes life can be so challenging that it seems meaningless. Every time I try to keep moving forward, it seems that I fall one step back. Help me to release these thoughts to You and to know in my heart of hearts that all of Your word is true so that I may be content and use this day to be and do all that You made me for. Use me to fulfill Your purpose. Amen"

Application Questions:

1. Are you blooming right now where God planted you?

2. If you're not blooming for Jesus in your life right now, why?

3. Do you believe God has a purpose for your life that is very significant to Him?

4. Will you be content in God today?

5. Do you trust Jesus to show you how to use your time and talents to glorify Him?

6. Whom can you encourage today that may feel they are insignificant?

7. Do your thoughts, actions, and attitudes glorify God daily in even the smallest ways?

Action Plan:

In order to "bloom where you are planted," first think about (and write down) all the areas you're "planted" in right now. These areas may include: career, church, ministry, a club you belong to, your neighborhood, and family – I think you get the idea. List at least five areas but try for ten or more. Next, list the three main ways you contribute to each of these areas already. For example, if your career is accounting you may put "service clients accounting needs, produce financial reports, support accounting team." Next, list a new contribution you can add that would have a positive, godly impact! The accountant may put "make a prayer list of coworkers and clients to pray for daily." Finally, start with one area of your life to add this new contribution and ask God to lead your efforts. You will be more fulfilled but more importantly, will honor God and bless others.

48

WHAT'S BLOCKING YOUR VIEW?

If you don't live a life of contented restraint, you're bound to suffer the exhaustion of gluttony.

Hebrews 4:13 "Nothing in all creation is hidden from God's sight. Everything is uncovered and laid bare before the eyes of him to whom we must give account."

Some years back I was attending a prayer meeting at the Tampa Bay Buccaneers' stadium office. After some intercessory prayer time, the keynote speaker, Wayne Huezinga, Jr., gave his personal testimony of growing up in one of America's richest families. Wayne's father built three Fortune 500 companies (Waste Management, Blockbuster Video, and Auto Nation).

After some years of rebellious living, Wayne, Jr. realized the emptiness in his life and accepted Christ as his Lord and Savior. It wasn't without a toll though. The rest of his family did not believe as he did, and many conflicts arose because of his commitment to Christ.

Not long after his conversion, a worker was at his house and reluctantly told Wayne God had given him a vision and he had been waiting for the right moment to share it. Now was the right moment. In broken English the worker shared his vision, and it heavily impacted Wayne's life.

The worker asked Wayne to hold a quarter in each hand between his thumb and first finger. He had him stretch his arms out so Wayne was seeing the President's pictures on the face of each coin. Then the worker stepped back 5 yards and said, "Pretend I am God and you are looking at me. Can you see God now?" Wayne answered, "Yes". The worker then asked Wayne to hold the quarters right in front of his eyes and asked the same question. This time Wayne's answer was "no." He could not see God; all he could see was the money.

The worker explained that if Wayne keeps his eyes on God and looks past the money, God will take care of him and the money. If he looks first at money instead of looking first at God he is in the wrong. That hit Wayne like a hammer over the head.

The same is true for all of us. We need to step back and consider what we are most focused on in life. If we are focused on anything other than God, Jesus Christ is taking second seat, and we have another God before Him. That's a huge problem because Jesus said if we put Him first, He will take care of our needs, but if we put anything else first, we are now our own provider and will soon find we are lacking the greatest things in life – faith, hope, and love. We will be left with the one thing we are focused on, which will one day also be gone if it's not Christ.

Prayer:

"Lord Jesus, I want You to be my one and only focus. Everything else that takes a priority is just a distraction that Satan tries to use to pull me away from you. Please show me what keeps me from seeing and hearing you clearly. Please help me remove anything that stands between You and me. You are my God and King, and I want only you to fill that spot in my life. Amen."

Application Questions:

1. What are you looking for first and foremost in your life?

2. Is there anything in your life you consider more important than Jesus Christ?

3. Do you look to God to provide in every area of your life?

4. What fear, worry, or desire takes your sights off God?

5. How clearly are you seeing and hearing God in your life?

6. Whom can you ask to inform you if they see anything blocking your focus on Jesus?

7. Are you willing to trust in God to remove those things that are blocking you from Him?

Action Plan:

Here is a simple exercise with a strong visual to help reinforce your priorities. Take your Bible, and set it in front of you so you can see it. Think about what that means to you, what Jesus means to you, and how important God is in your life. Now, think about other things in your life that you spend time and energy on. It could be family, finances, career, hobbies, or anything else that comes to mind. Consider those areas, and then think about something tangible that represents them (like your checkbook for finances, a picture of your family, or a plaque from work). Consider the symbol for each area and how you would rank it in priority to the Bible in front of you. Would you put each object on top of the Bible representing that it takes priority for you, or would you place your Bible (as the only supreme priority) on top of anything you can think of? If there is anything you would place above God and the Bible, search your heart this next week and ask God to lead you in learning how to put Him as top priority in your life.

49 MAKING TOUGH DECISIONS

The only decision that really matters is the one you make.

Hebrews 11:6 "... without faith it is impossible to please God, because anyone who comes to him must believe that he exists and that he rewards those who earnestly seek him."

We have all had to make hard decisions in life, decisions that impact not only us, but also the people around us. People we care about and are even related to. So how do you make your decision? Sometimes the tough decision is obvious, and although we may not want to do it, we know it is the best choice. Other times God leads us to make tough and challenging decisions based strictly on one thing – faith in Him! Those are the most testing, most challenging, and most fulfilling situations in life.

I remember moving to California several years back, which was a very hard decision. It required me to leave my security, job, family, friends, and a great place to live, and going to a "foreign land" where I knew no one and had no job. All I heard about California was that it was the "granola state" (filled with fruits, nuts, and flakes). The only truth I had to go on in making the decision was my faith that God was truly leading me there.

I could have easily shrunk back by listening to all the opinions around me, which told me not to move. I could have dwelled on my lack of finances. I could have taken a good look at my car (a 10 year old Ford Escort with mechanical problems) that was supposed to get me there, and I could have turned back in fear. I had nothing solid waiting for me in California, yet after fasting and several hours with my face buried in the carpet at the front of our church, I felt God's direction through peace. I decided to do the hard thing, and God confirmed it with a note I received from a stranger. While I was sitting in church next to a woman I had not seen before nor after, she slipped me a piece of paper during the service that said "God is moving on your behalf" then smiled at me, as if to say "take the step of faith." It ended up being one of the best decisions of my life.

By leaving my comfort zone, I found California was the place for me to live. I met some of the most Godly and wholesome people living in California. I also got to train with some of the best athletes in the world and advance my career skills to an even higher level. Most important of all – I found my other half.

The truly great men and women of faith have to make tough decisions – Moses, Noah, Jonah, David, Rahab, and others. If you are going to be a person whose story would be included in the Bible (if it were still being written today), you must seek God's direction with all your heart (even it if takes hours face down in prayer) to stand in faith by following Him in tough decisions!

Prayer:
"Lord Jesus, I want to glorify You in all I say and do. I want Your will to be the only thing I base my decisions on. Use me, mold me, and shape me into being more like You day by day. Speak to me, Lord, and show me how to make tough decisions that may not even make sense to me, but you will use for your glory. I stand on Your Word to follow your Holy Spirit."

Application Questions:

1. What is a tough decision you have faced in the past couple years?

2. What tough decision are you facing now?

3. How did you pursue God to know His will in the matter?

4. How much time are you willing to spend in prayer to know God's plan?

5. How do you use (if at all) fasting in your life to search for God's will?

6. Putting aside other's opinions and your worries, what is God calling you to do?

7. Who is a person in your life that will pray and support you to follow God's will?

Action Plan:

Take one day this next week to spend special quiet time of at least 30 minutes with Jesus. You will need to go to a quiet place in your house or in your neighborhood. I personally love to be near water at a local lake or beach. Have blank paper and a pen with you. During these 30 minutes take time to quiet your mind! You can do this by focusing on Jesus. Picture His face, think of scriptures, and ask Him to calm you. For me to release all the commotion in my mind to really hear God, it takes about 20 minutes. It may be a little longer or shorter for you. Once your mind really quiets and you feel the peace from the Lord, ask Him to speak to you. He will normally do this by putting ideas and/or pictures in your mind. Capture what you see and hear. This can be a life-changing experience for you. Then make sure to set aside time in your schedule to do this more consistently.

50 BEING A CHRISTIAN

As Christians we get caught up in 'how' to be a good Christian and lose perspective on 'why'

Proverbs 29:18 "Without vision people perish."

If you have never been to the Smithsonian Institute in Washington D.C., it is well worth the trip. One of my favorite museums there is the Air and Space Museum. On the most recent trip we took there, I appreciated it even more because if it weren't for aviation, we wouldn't have had enough time to drive up to D.C. to see the museum

I am fascinated by flight, and at the museum I spent time studying the two brothers who are credited with the first flight – Wilbur and Orville Wright. Although they faced much adversity, they had a vision and incredible persistence to pursue the vision, which I believe was God given ("Without vision, people perish").

So I asked myself the question, "Why were these two brothers successful when so many others before them were not?" The main difference I discovered was they approached flying differently than everyone else. Instead of trying to learn "how" to fly, they studied to learn "why" flight happens. These brothers studied the results of everyone's testing (including their own) to understand "why" flight with birds, or anything else, actually works. By discovering "why," they learned "how" to develop the first plane to ever actually fly, and they changed the world.

I once heard a powerful quote from Zig Ziglar that says, "If the why is strong enough, the how will happen." For the Wright Brothers not only was their "why" strong enough, but it placed in them a great conviction, passion, hope, and perseverance to achieve their vision.

When it comes to living the Christian life and following Jesus, if we are more focused on the "how" rather than the "why," we will never get our spiritual wings off the ground. Trying to figure out how to live correctly, how to please God, and how to earn God's favor will get the same results of all those who tried to fly before the Wright Brothers. However, if we focus on why we accepted Christ in the first place, it will change our lives. Focus on God's pure love for us as his children, His enduring mercy to not give us what we deserve for sinning, and His grace to give us the great blessings we don't deserve in life. His "why" is strong enough so our "how" will happen!

Prayer:

"Lord God, help me trust You more in my life. Help me to be the person You want me to be instead of trying to always do things to please others. I know the answer to all my questions lie in Your Word and truth. Help me to discern the true reasons "why" You love me and want me to love others and "why" I am here on this earth today. I know You will show me how all of these things work together for Your purpose. Amen"

Application Questions:

1. In what areas of your Christian walk do you focus more on the "how" than on the "why"?

2. Why is it important for you to love God?

3. Why is it important for you to love others?

4. Why does God have you here on this earth today?

5. For what purpose are you living each day?

6. How do you describe the difference between the "how's" and "why's" of your life?

7. Who can help you clarify the "why" so the "how" will become clearer?

Action Plan:

Here are some key areas to review to determine if you live based more on the "how" or on the "why" of Christ. Think about when you first came to Christ, and consider why you chose to surrender your life and ask Jesus to be your Lord. Was it because His love and forgiveness drew you to Him and gave you hope? It probably was not because you felt you had to do lots of work to earn Christ's love and forgiveness. Since that day when you asked Christ to be your Savior, did your main focus shift from "why" you're saved to "how" best to live your life, be successful, help others, or whatever other focus? There is nothing wrong in pursuing these things if they are driven by the "why" of your life. If you are drawing close to God daily and He is leading you in "how" to pursue his purpose for you - perfect! If you are focused on the "how's" of life where God is only a part of your life yet He is not the "why" that leads your daily activities it's time to get back to the original reason you accepted Christ as your Savior.

51

FIGHT VERSUS FLIGHT

When to stand up and fight versus when to humbly surrender determines your destiny in life!

Ephesians 6:12 "For our struggle is not against flesh and blood, but against the rulers, against the authorities, against the powers of this dark world and against the spiritual forces of evil in the heavenly realms."

It can be difficult to handle all the areas of this thing called "life." We can go to church, pray, and spend time with God and know His word, but when life happens – right here, right now in "real time," what is the best way to handle each situation? The sports and business worlds tell us to fight for everything we want. But then we look at the life of Jesus. He simply surrendered His very life without even considering fighting the religious leaders of the day – or did He?

There are two popular Christian songs that stand in seemingly direct contrast to each other: "All to Jesus I Surrender" and "Onward Christian Soldier". How to balance these two opposites in life is a huge key to our walk with God. When do we fight and when do we take flight? The answer lies in God's truth. A new Christian once said to me, "The hardest part I find about being a Christian is surrendering everything to God!" That was one of the wisest things I have heard anyone say! In this world we are called by God to both surrender and to fight.

It seems as if we end up fighting God in many areas of our lives. That is in direct contrast to God's call to surrender everything to Him. We can be fighting God by having a bad attitude, by holding a grudge, or simply by not doing what He calls us to. As Christians our way of life should always be about willingly surrendering everything to Him. It's all His anyway! Everything includes your health, thoughts, goals, dreams, family, friends, career, finances, and everything else you can think of. Just like Jesus, we should make it our priority to turn every thought, worry, and struggle over to God! You will one day leave it all here anyway. It's much better to willingly hand it over now than have God pry it away from you.

So if you really do surrender to God, where is the need to fight? Simple – you are already in a battle every moment of every day, whether you want to be or not. A war is fiercely being waged against you in your mind. If you are a Christian, you must fight. The first and most important fight is against the thoughts that come into your mind. The second is actions you take in the physical world. Jesus battled Satan with scripture, and in the physical world he battled the religion, corruption, and evils of His day. Surrender to every God motivation, and battle all others. You must do this by standing on God's Word and promises, then by physically doing what's right, and finally by confronting evil through love.

Prayer:

"Lord Jesus, I bow down to You in complete surrender. I give You all that I am, all that I have, all that I think, and all that I do. Help me to know Your truth and live by it. Help me to battle the lies of Satan and to stand up for Your truth in love and conviction. Amen"

Application Questions:

1. How well have you surrendered everything to God today?

2. How well do you surrender to God every day?

3. How well are you battling lies with truth in your mind?

4. How well are you battling lies with truth in your actions?

5. Are you studying and memorizing God's Word and promises on a daily basis?

6. How well do you understand God's truth to know how and what to fight for?

7. Who is an accountability partner that can encourage you to surrender and to fight?

Action Plan:

One of the hardest things to do as a Christian is surrender all. What areas in your life are the hardest to surrender to Jesus? Spend your next quiet time in prayer asking God to help you surrender these challenging areas to Him. To get to the place of full surrender may take days, weeks, months, or more of continually turning areas over to God until it becomes natural and automatic. The challenge, you may find, is your pride. It may try to put up a good fight because we want to fight back, get the credit for something, or do it ourselves. Surrender these ambitions to God then do what He calls you to do. He may even call you to stand up and fight. There may be times God will do this in your life by having you stand up for your beliefs or for someone else, or by having you confront a leader, etc. The key here is to make sure that your actions are led by God. A good story to read about both "surrender" and the "fight" that ensued is the book of Esther.

52 KNOW THAT YOU KNOW

Are you really who you appear to be to other people?

Matthew 25:21 "His master replied, 'well done, good and faithful servant! You have been faithful with a few things; I will put you in charge of many things. Come and share your master's happiness!'"

I talk a lot about the importance of having support in life especially in the form of mentors, coaches, and accountability partners. I believe so strongly in these types of relationships that I established my career as a coach to help hundreds, and now thousands, of people in all areas of life! However, I didn't just become a coach on a whim. It became a passion for me because of the tremendous influence other mentors had on me.

In 2004 I finally got to meet the most impactful man in my life (other than Jesus). I flew to Cleveland so I could attend one of our company's seminars at the Gund Arena. This time I wasn't there to work, but to meet my mentor Zig Ziglar in person. If you don't know who Zig is, he is an incredible teacher and motivational speaker who has been used by God to change millions of lives – including mine. I strongly recommend reading or listening to his material. The book of his that greatly impacted my life is Over the Top.

I considered Zig to be a mentor because of what he taught me through his books and recordings. After meeting him I now also consider him a friend. Zig is genuine! Zig is the same person on and off stage. Unfortunately not all other popular speakers are like this. At 77 years old, all he talked about was his love for God, his wife, and his continual desire to help others. The passion in his eyes was unmistakable.

After 45 minutes with Zig, I was extremely moved. I called my wife and just started crying. I couldn't hold back the tears. God has used this man to change my life over the years, and our initial conversation was so impactful that I couldn't control my emotions. I decided my goal in life would be to impact others as deeply and profoundly with God's love as I could, just as Zig does.

That day Zig shared many things with me that were powerful including the struggles he faced over the years, but he never gave up. However, there is one thing he said that still gives me chills to think about. He looked me straight in the eye and said, "Brian, I know that I know that I know that I am doing exactly what God called me to do, and I will do that until the day I leave this earth." This is how all Christians should live! Thank you, Zig, for setting the example.

Prayer:

"Lord Jesus, I love you. You are the most genuine person who ever walked the face of the earth. Please forgive me. I know I am not perfect and I ask that You help me to live righteously all areas of life. I want to be used by You. I pray You use me to impact all others around me for the purpose of your Kingdom. Thank you Lord. Amen."

 **Application Questions:**

1. Are there areas in your life where you put on a mask to the world and hide behind it?

2. Have you come clean with God today and asked for a renewed heart?

3. Do you have any mentors in your life that actually live a life of righteousness?

4. Can you say right now, "I know that I know I am doing exactly what I'm called to do"?

5. What do you need to do or change to be completely in line with God's plan?

6. Do you have anyone you can share your needs and burdens with?

7. Whom are you helping to walk closer with God and to fulfill His calling?

Action Plan:

Think of Zig Ziglar's statement: "I know that I know that I know that I am doing exactly what God called me to do." How do you feel about that? If you can say this for yourself today, excellent! Continue to follow God's plan until the day you go to be with Him. If you cannot say this, here are some steps to start with. First you need to know God's purpose for your life. A couple of resources that can help you with this are *The Purpose Driven Life* by Rick Warren and *Only You Can Be You* by Eric Rees. If you already know the career or mission God has called you to, but aren't there yet, write down exactly what that purpose is. Next, take a couple days to pray about this and ask Jesus to confirm it. As you pray, assess in writing where you are now, where you want to be, and what you would need to change to get there. A great resource that can help at this stage is Zig Ziglar's *The Performance Planner*. Keep in mind it may take you time to actually get to the spot God has shown you; it took me decades. However, in the process you should live each day doing what God is calling you to do. In the process, make sure you have Christian mentors, coaches, and accountability partners in your life to support you.

Made in the USA
Coppell, TX
10 May 2021